IS THERE
MORE?

Praise for Is There More? Resurrecting Communion

This book speaks to the heart of an important topic that deserves more attention.

NEWT GINGRICH, 50th Speaker of the U.S. House of Representatives

David Warnick, my friend of thirty years, a man of deep devotion and love for God; his communion in the Lord's Supper will cause you to draw near to the Lord's heart and be swept into the beauty of His righteousness. Read it and be blessed!

LOU ENGLE, Founder of *The Call* prayer movement
Author, *Digging the Wells of Revival* and *The Call of the Elijah Revolution*

Have you ever wondered if you're missing something when you receive communion? Have you felt like there's something more for you in the Lord's Supper? This book is for you. David Warnick does a masterful job of unfolding aspects of the Lord's purpose and heart when He instructed us to remember Him in this act. The stories and examples in this book will grow your passion for Jesus.

MIKE BICKLE, International House of Prayer of Kansas City

Even when we were young and active in politics together, David and Nikki Warnick's friends admired their special lives of true faith. Now David has written a book on communion—clear, sharp and full of original insights for believers of all backgrounds.

KARL ROVE, Senior White House Advisor to George W. Bush

Throughout history the Church has lost her way. The vibrancy of our communities and the poignancy of our creeds have, at times, been emptied by our lack of expectancy, obedience, and wonder at the majesty of God. In mercy, God raises up voices who help us rediscover the glories hidden by our own wandering. David Warnick is such a voice. My hope is that *Is There More?* can help the Church find her way back to a joyful, transactional, and life-giving experience of the Lord's Supper. May we return to our place at the Lord's Table and recover the context in which our cup overflows!

ADAM NARCISO, Pioneer and Visionary,
Catalyst Ministries, Nashville

David Warnick's passion for Jesus Christ is something which always inspires me.

MARK ELSDON-DEW, Communications Director,
Holy Trinity Brompton, London
Author: *The God Who Changes Lives*

We are all familiar with the Lord's Supper and the act of taking communion at church services. But what if there is more to the Lord's Supper than we understand? What if God wants to reveal to us a deeper understanding of the symbolic act when we break bread and drink from the cup? David Warnick's new book is a biblically sound exposition of the Lord's Supper and His command to "do this in remembrance of Me" (1 Cor. 11:24–25). I believe that if you open your heart and mind to what David presents in the pages ahead, you will receive an impartation of knowledge that will take you to another level of understanding, intimacy, and fellowship with our Lord Jesus and one another. I highly recommend this book!

DR. CHÉ AHN, Founding Pastor, HRock Church, Pasadena
President, Harvest International Ministry
Author of several books, including
Say Goodbye to Powerless Christianity

This will strengthen your relationship with Jesus. Communion has been lost in the religious acts of the church. This book brings it all to the surface, makes us think of why we take communion, and the importance of it. This author provides clarity in why we do what we do, and the real importance of what we do and why we do it.

PASTOR TIM D. REMINGTON,
Founder, Good Samaritan Rehabilitation, Idaho
Featured on *The 700 Club* after miraculously surviving
six close-range .45 caliber pistol shots

This examination of the Lord's Supper is just what we need to help us to be obedient to this basic command of Christ. This book succinctly and insightfully addresses the common issues that keep us from basic obedience to Jesus. It will be a book I highly recommend to those in our training who have concerns about celebrating the Lord's Supper. It's immensely practical and theologically informed—a great balance for those of us who love Jesus but don't want to read abstract theological tomes either! I would recommend this book to all.

DR. PAM ARLUND, International Leadership Team, All Nations
Author, *Pocket Guide to Church Planting*

My dear friend David Warnick challenges and helps us all to reflect on the meaning and practice of the Lord's Supper, whatever our Christian tradition. His Edinburgh University teacher and mine, who sent him on his quest to understand the Supper those decades ago, would have called it a converting ordinance, so named in the Scottish communion tradition. David opens up this rich evangelistic understanding of the Supper and its converting power for many outside our Scottish tradition in fresh and enlivening ways.

WILLIAM STORRAR, minister of the Church of Scotland and former Professor of Practical Theology at the University of Edinburgh

In the early church, communion was an integral expression of community life. Initially the disciples were defensive of their newfound faith and practice. Many paid with their life for following Jesus. So it was vital for them to keep the centrality of their community life. In Acts Chapter 2 it is evident that this practice was integral to the practice of the Christian faith. Through the years, the practice has taken different modes, but essentially the centrality of this teaching remains. David is a meticulous writer and has produced this in all simplicity. I commend this to wider reading.

J. VARADARAJ, Senior Minister, India

David's insights into the Lord's Supper are refreshing. I'd encourage you to dive head first into *Is There More?* so that your soul is strengthened.

This book will draw you closer to our Creator in ways you've never imagined. Do yourself a favor and glean from David's revelations on the subject on communion.

JOHN O'SHAUGHNESSY, Praiseworthy Ministry
Author, *Keys to Understanding*

David Warnick has written, with sage wisdom and fresh insights, about the Christian tradition's oldest practice: The Lord's Supper. Regardless of your background or experience in taking The Lord's Supper, you will be encouraged to celebrate the benefits of participating in this sacred practice more often after reading his book. For too long we have abdicated our role in teaching our children the privilege and importance of regularly memorializing our Lord through The Lord's Supper. It is my hope that this book and your commitment to re-engage the essence of the Christian faith in your home through this practice would be the basis for the spiritual renewal in our households, both natural and spiritual.

KEN CANFIELD, Founder, National Center for Fathering
Author, *Seven Secrets of Effective Fathering* and *The Heart of a Father*

This is a comprehensive study of the Lord's Supper with a fresh approach. Rather than a seminary textbook approach, the author explores this subject with a community context in mind, as in New Testament times. He examines twenty-four issues of the Lord's Supper from all angles—biblical, historical, and experiential. Well-done!

JOHN WESLEY "WES" ADAMS, Ph.D.
Coauthor and editor of *The Fire Bible* (formerly *The Full Life Study Bible*)

I am grateful to David Warnick for his excellent work on the Lord's Supper. For many years I have felt that there is so much more to the practice of what we refer to as communion than we often experience. David encourages us to think afresh and come to Lord's Table with a sense of expectancy.

REV. DR. ROY PATTON, former Moderator,
Presbyterian Church in Ireland

IS THERE MORE?

RESURRECTING COMMUNION

DAVID WARNICK

Is There More? Resurrecting Communion
© 2018 by David Warnick
Published by Deep River Books
Sisters, Oregon

www.deepriverbooks.com

ISBN – 13: 9781632694768

LOC: 2018946984

Printed in the USA
Cover Design by Connie Gabbert

TABLE OF CONTENTS

ACKNOWLEDGMENTS

WITH GRATEFUL ACKNOWLEDGMENTS to my wife Nikki; my children A. J., John, Joshua, Kateri, and Grace; and our church family—it is both a truism and trite to say how much you mean to me. But I trust you can receive my words as more than a clichè—just as I want our Lord's Supper to be!

Let me acknowledge the late John Gray, my Christian Education professor at the University of Edinburgh, for a comment that kept me thinking on this topic for years: that the Reformers saw communion as evangelistic. Let me honor four friends who've passed on—Don Carmichael, Glenn Miles, Brian Pugh, and Greg Truty—for their encouragement in different ways. My deep thanks to Richard Slimbach for fanning the flames; to Robert Bierman for first suggesting I write these thoughts down; to Mark Elsdon-Dew, Michael Kailus, Rob Morrissette, Gerard Beigel, George Patterson, and Dierk Mueller for their crucial advice; and Kathi DeCanio for her help. Thank you to Les and Alexis Howard, and Lex and Cindi Ferguson, for your amazing support over the months. Thank you to my lead pastor, Geoffrey Winkler, and before him Gary Fox, and to our church body, for providing the context to develop these thoughts (and Geoffrey for your marketing help).

Thank you to the wonderful folks at Deep River Books, starting with Andy Carmichael (special thanks for helping me close in on a title and finding Connie Gabbert), Bill and Nancie Carmichael, Bev Tucker, Alexis Miller, Tamara Barnet, Carl Simmons, and the other team members!

Thank you to Melissa Thiringer for her proofreading help. A special thanks to Colin Symes and Rich Stone for their enthusiasm when I was weary of pursuing this subject. Let me close by saying that I can't adequately express how indebted I am to the late John Sandford for his interest and passion for this topic, as well as unity within the body of Christ.

With many thanks for His grace,

David Warnick

Coeur d'Alene, Idaho

FOREWORD

THE FIRST TIME I read the Gospels, a few scenes struck me as pure genius. The Lord's Supper was one of them. When Jesus introduced this simple practice to His disciples He illustrated the heart of the gospel in a way that would never be forgotten. The Lord's Supper is literally the gospel in miniature form, summarizing the very heart of God for humankind.

Jesus introduced the communion supper in the setting of fellow believers, His disciples, with Himself as the main focus. This simple practice simultaneously points to Jesus' past acts of sacrificial love, His presence in the community of believers, and the future wedding supper of the Lamb. Jesus is truly the same yesterday, today, and forever!

In this book, David Warnick asks us to reconsider how we think about communion. Do we approach communion merely as a spiritual exercise or are we participating in our Lord's promises? His answer will surprise you.

David's greatest challenge for me, and possibly for you, is to examine the importance we place on the Lord's Supper. Do we value it based on the benefits derived from following this action or is it important to us because the Lord values it?

The value Jesus placed on communion can be understood by looking at His points of emphasis. Jesus said, "Do this in remembrance of *me*." In so doing, we remember His wonderful acts of sacrificial love and all the benefits that flow from it. More importantly, we are to remember *Him*. He is to be worshipped for who He is, and who He is supersedes all the acts He has ever done. In John 15, Jesus stated his followers were not servants but friends—a statement showing us that His desire is to commune with us.

In line with that desire, David seeks to live a life of love and obedience to Jesus. It is in this spirit that he investigates the current practice of the Lord's Supper. His penetrating questions help remove any vagueness surrounding the Lord's Supper, thrusting it back into a vital faith encounter. His book will ignite your heart with passion, changing the Lord's Supper from a Christian ritual into a heartfelt reality. My view of the Lord's Supper will forever be changed.

Clifford Baker
Mighty in Spirit Ministries
Author, *Come Away My Love*

INTRODUCTION

I WEAR GLASSES. I know that if the lenses are wrong, I won't see things right. And at the same time, my glasses affect how others see me. Communion is like a set of glasses for our Christian life. If the lenses aren't right, it will distort our whole life in Christ. And it will also affect how others see the faith.

For instance, sharing communion is a request for all of us, from our big brother Jesus. Yet are we eager to initiate obeying Him ourselves? Are we always waiting for someone else to guide our obedience?

Or again, do we view it as something we do together, as joint-owners of a family business having a reunion—or like an assignment we're doing as a worker carrying out a job description? Are we approaching communion as employees, or as children?

This book aims to take you from where communion is individualistic, solemn, and restricted, to a joyful and community-breathing event.

I started my own journey wondering about communion, or the Lord's Supper, because:

- The way we do it has changed dramatically from the way Jesus's first followers did it.
- Our focus today seems to be more on ourselves and our condition, than on the Lord and His finished work.
- And, perhaps because of this, I see that our emotional tone during the Supper is usually more somber than joyful, and our social tone more isolated than connected.

We need to change the relational context, the emotional tone, and the spiritual focus. If you look at the passages in Acts, 1 Corinthians, and Jude, we see there's no distinction between what we'd know as a church covered-dish meal and the ceremony of communion. The remembrance of the Lord was part of a party! The emotional tone is joy; Acts 2 says they broke bread with gladness and sincerity of heart. And tied to that: The focus wasn't inward, on our individual spiritual condition, but upward on the goodness of God.

What would happen if we take communion seriously, and not just leave it as "the hole in the service"? (That's a term I understand at least one leader used in talking about communion.) I believe there's a third way—an alternative between how some have taken it seriously but made it a ceremony without connecting us with each other in joy, and others who've tried to explain it in natural terms or dumbed communion down and left it as an add-on. We can move toward unity in the body of Christ—including those who honor tradition and those who honor the New Testament. We can arrive at the same place if we accept the pattern in the New Testament, which after all, is our oldest tradition.

The early church celebrated communion as part of a meal. That's a different context than almost any practiced today. What would happen if we all went back to that?

There was no requirement in the early church for a leader with ordained authority to lead communion. Once believers accept that any one of us can take initiative and invite other believers to participate in the body and blood of the Lord, we can see practical unity emerge in the way the church approaches communion.

Once we accept that when Jesus gave a command to "remember Him" and that any person can respond to His command, we'll open up communion to all those present.

Once we accept that His words—"This is my body"—are true, regardless of how we mentally explain or understand them, then we can move toward practical unity in our faith and practice. It is possible we can bring communion back to life.

The book begins with a fantasy, a dream of what might be possible if we open up to all our Lord has for us in the action of communion. Then we'll look at the different threads that need to be woven together for the dream to come to pass. Often I start looking at each thread, each topic, from my mistaken thinking and then present the correction. We'll look at two dozen aspects of communion (or, as Paul terms it, the Lord's Supper, and I'll use both terms interchangeably). It'll be like looking at the back side of a tapestry. Then—voilà —the story in the postscript will return us to the front of the tapestry. For those who want specific suggestions, check out Appendix 3, "What Could It Be Like?"

COULD THIS FANTASY BECOME REAL?

I t was a small wedding. I knew the groom reasonably well from work, and I was willing to go through the ordeal of meeting some strangers to be part of his big day. Besides, for all I knew, there'd be some good food at the reception.

I haven't been to a lot of these ceremonies—most of my friends don't go in for them—but still there seemed to be something different about this one, even from the beginning. But for me, it really got strange . . . well, "strange" isn't quite the right word. Interesting? No, intense—maybe that's the best word I can think of: intense. It got intense when the man up front said that the bride and groom wanted to invite everyone to share in communion, or "the Lord's Supper."

Now I think I'd been at a couple of weddings in the past where the bride and groom did something like that by themselves up front, but I'd never been invited to be part of it! I wasn't sure what to do, but it became obvious in a minute. A couple of the attendants passed around a basket with chunks of sourdough bread in it—and the person next to me took one, so I did too. Then another couple of attendants brought a tray with small cups of grape juice around, so I took one of those.

Then the man up front explained that we, as friends of the bride and groom, were really more than just spectators. We were connected to them—in the same way all these pieces of bread had been part of one loaf. Then he explained that Jesus said the loaf of bread was His body—and that everyone connected with Him is also part of His body. He said something about how we were all invited to be part of what Jesus had done by dying on the cross. That was a little hard to follow, but what was even harder to explain was what happened when I bit into that piece of bread.

I guess the best way of explaining it is to say it's like the yeast or something in that bread exploded inside my mouth and then warmed my insides all the way down. But the experience wasn't over yet. I drank down that little cup— and yet it's like all that did was give me a greater thirst. I wanted it again. In fact, over the next week the feeling kept coming back—and yet I knew it wasn't particularly the drink I wanted; it was something else.

Nothing seemed to change for everyone else, the ceremony just went on. The bride and groom said vows, and exchanged rings, and there was a musical number. But honestly, I missed most of what was said, because I was still in some sort of trance. The couple kissed and there was cheering, and after a while the reception got under way. I was moving pretty much in slow motion, waiting, and finally I got a moment with the groom.

It was just the two of us, so I felt comfortable asking: "What was in that bread?"

I knew I wanted it again!

CHAPTER 1

IS COMMUNION ALL IN THE HEAD?

I used to think communion was just a mental exercise.
Now, I know we're participating
in the objective reality of our Lord's promises.

ONE NIGHT I STAYED at an unfamiliar lodge. I worked late, and after going to sleep I had a troubled dream—I'd lost my organizer! Those who know me would tell you that "organ-izer" is an apt description—it's like an additional part of my body. I'm lost without my calendar, my contacts, and my "to-do" list. I was panicked! What was I going to do? How could I go on? Even now, the anxiety that dream created affects my pulse.

Then I woke up, and I saw the desk, and my organizer on it—and peace settled over me. I *remembered* where I really was.

When I think of it: Isn't this like our "remembering" in the Lord's Supper?

We're waking up to reality—reminding ourselves where we really are—who's really right beside us—what's really going on and what the real value of things and people are. *This remembrance isn't to emphasize our distance from the historical event of the Cross, but rather the nearness of the rule and reign of God.* I realize afresh that no matter what's going on, no matter what's around me, if I stop breathing I'll enter our Lord's rule and reign in a few minutes. His kingship will be complete, for me, at that moment! That's how close He is to each of us.

For many years I had mistakenly thought I was the one who gave the action of the Lord's Supper meaning. My mistaken thinking did grow from a biblical source—and as we look further, we'll see our mental involvement does matter in how we *experience* the reality of the event—but it doesn't affect the reality of the event.

I thought the focus of the Lord's Supper was on what I was thinking and feeling because I misunderstood Jesus' instructions:

> For I received from the Lord what I also delivered to you, that the Lord Jesus on the night when he was betrayed took bread, and when he had given thanks, he broke it, and said, "This is my body which is for you. Do this in remembrance of me.[1]

"Remembering" is a peculiar activity. "Remembrance" can seem to emphasize our distance from an event. It can emphasize how long ago something happened. Thus, our focus can be on our mental effort to recall, trying hard to focus on something.

But I'd suggest remembering during the Lord's Supper is like waking up from a dream. It's recalling reality.

Still, the Lord's Supper is more than this type of "remembering." The Supper is something much more.

I didn't understand that "much more"—and I suspect there have been believers in generations past who didn't either. For instance, consider a book my mother passed on to me from her godly father's library. It's more than three hundred years old. It talks about the problem the author, Edmund Calamy, saw with people's approach to the Lord's Supper:

> [W]hen they come to it [the Lord's Supper], they endeavour to think affectionately of His Incarnation, Passion and Crucifixion and thus far indeed 'tis well: But while they stop here and go no further, they leave out a main

---

1   1 Corinthians 11:23–24, ESV.

thing: which lies in the Covenant Transaction between
their God and Savior and them.[2]

"Aha," I thought as I read this, "He's describing me. I'm the person
who 'endeavors to think affectionately of His incarnation, passion, and
crucifixion.'" Calamy goes on to describe what I'm missing—that the
Lord's Supper is a *transaction* where God refreshes our experience of His
covenant with us. The Bible puts it this way: "The cup of blessing that we
bless, is it not a participation in the blood of Christ? The bread that we
break, is it not a participation in the body of Christ?"[3]

It's a "participation," or a "sharing"—or a "communion." Since "communion" has come to be the name of the act of "the Lord's Supper," let's
use another word to better convey the meaning: The Lord's Supper is a
"communication." Some will bring up the question: "What happens to the
bread and cup?"[4] Paul's words point beyond a focus on the elements to the
overall interaction.

When we join together to share the bread and cup we allow God's
kingship, the supernatural realm, to penetrate more into our hearts.
That's "participation" in the blood and body of Christ. For those who
view belief and faith as something that's strictly mental, this may be
hard to grasp. C. S. Lewis puts it this way talking about his experience of
communion:

---

2   Edmund Calamy, *A Practical Discourse Concerning Vows with A Special Reference
to Baptism and the Lord's Supper*, (London: Geo. Larkin, 1697), 97. Calamy is
the grandson of an English pastor of the same name who was a member of the
Westminster Assembly that wrote the Westminster Confession. The grandson
"acquired a reputation as the biographer of the ejected clergy [the 2,000 pastors
ejected from the Church of England by the Act of Conformity]. He was born in
London, April 5, 1671, educated among the Dissenters and in Holland (1688-9);
was pastor in London, 1692, and died there June 3, 1732. He was held in high
regard." *The New International Encyclopedia*, (New York: Dodd, Mead and Com-
pany, 1903), Vol. III, 738.
3   1 Corinthians 10:16, NABre.
4   For a summary of different views see Chapter 14, "Con or non, trans up or down?"

I find no difficulty in believing that the veil between the worlds, nowhere else (for me) so opaque to the intellect, is nowhere else so thin and permeable to divine operation. Here a hand from the hidden country touches not only my soul but my body.[5]

Let me suggest that it's the total package of joining together and eating and drinking the Lord's Supper—involving body, mind, and spirit—that distills the Lord's presence for us.

What do I mean by "distilling the Lord's presence"? Isn't the Lord everywhere? After all, Psalm 139 says: "Where can I go from your Spirit? Where can I flee from your presence?"[6] But Elijah's chronicler records:

And behold, the LORD passed by, and a great and strong wind tore the mountains and broke in pieces the rocks before the LORD, but the LORD was not in the wind. And after the wind an earthquake, but the LORD was not in the earthquake. And after the earthquake a fire, but the LORD was not in the fire.[7]

If the Lord is described as "not in" something, it means that there must be some diminution of His presence, even if He's not entirely absent.

There are other passages describing our Lord's presence. Jesus said, just before He departed by ascending into the sky, "And behold, I am with you always, until the end of the age."[8] Some aspect of Jesus' presence is always constant in believers' lives. The implication of Jesus' words that

5   C. S. Lewis, *Letters to Malcolm: Chiefly on Prayer* (New York: Harcourt Brace Jovanovich, 1964), 103.

6   Psalm 139:7, NIV.

7   1 Kings 19:11b–12a, ESV.

8   Matthew 28:20, NABre.

it was good for his followers that he went away;[9] is that His presence after His departure would be of a higher quality, a more intimate connection, than even physically being present with people before His crucifixion. But, even that enhanced type of presence must be of a different quality than the kind Paul describes as following our physical death:

> So *we are* always confident, knowing that while we are at home in the body we are absent from the Lord. For we walk by faith, not by sight. We are confident, yes, well pleased rather to be absent from the body and to be present with the Lord.[10]

Some translations use a different term in the last phrase, "and we would rather be away from the body and at home with the Lord."[11] Still, this type of presence following our physical death appears to be different than another presence which is described with a similar term, that of "dwelling":

> In him you also are being built together into a *dwelling place for God* by the Spirit.[12]
> That he may grant you in accord with the riches of his glory to be strengthened with power through his Spirit in the inner self, and that Christ may dwell in your hearts through faith; that you, rooted and grounded in love, . . .[13]

When Paul speaks of the Lord's Supper, he distinguishes two types of presence—"This is My body" is one kind of presence; "until He comes" is another. Jesus' coming is distinct and more complete than the bread

---

9   John 16:7.
10   2 Corinthians 5:6–8, NKJV.
11   2 Corinthians 5:8b, ESV. "Home" is also used in the NIV and NABre.
12   Ephesians 2:22, ESV, emphasis added.
13   Ephesians 3:16–17, NABre.

and the cup. The bread and the cup can be seen in Paul's words as a precursor of the fullness of His coming.

How can we put these different kinds of presence into a coherent picture? I'd suggest that the "everywhere-presence"[14] of God referred to in Psalm 139 is similar to the presence of water vapor in our atmosphere. We can't see it—but it's there. Then when the temperature and conditions are right, the vapor condenses and becomes liquid. We can see it physically at that point. The vapor becomes dew or rain. In fact, there's a predictability to the process—condensation follows a pattern. In a similar way, our Lord becomes more tangible, His presence more like a "dwelling presence," when certain conditions exist. For instance, His presence when "two or three" come together in His name,[15] or when we participate in His body and blood! We feel His presence powerfully but cannot see Him physically.

The effects of the Lord's Supper are more than the total of all the human responses involved—because the Lord is participating. Here's a mental picture: As I share the bread, I'm throwing a rock in a puddle—there are ripples. But to make the picture more accurate, we need to picture another rock thrown in simultaneously—by our Lord Himself. And

---

14 I use the word "everywhere-presence" of God, rather than the more usual "omnipresence" for two reasons. First, to remind us that the Bible doesn't use those philosophical terms in describing God. In fact, the Bible says there are "places" God can't be, at least in some sense: "For you are not a God who delights in wickedness; evil may not dwell with you" (Psalm 5:4, ESV). Second, to focus on "presence" as referring to location, to the "whereness" of being. C. S. Lewis shares my concern about using "omnipresence": "It also blurs the distinctions, the truth that God is present in each thing but not necessarily in the same mode; not in a man as in the consecrated bread and wine, not in a bad man as in a good one, nor in a beast as in a man . . . there is a paradox here. The higher the creature, the more and also the less, God is in it; the more present by grace, and the less present (by a sort of abdication) as mere power." Lewis, *Letters to Malcolm* (New York: Harcourt Brace Jovanovich, 1964), 74.

15 Matthew 18:19. Although it's quoted and may apply in many other situations, this passage is in the context of church discipline, of Jesus' followers calling a fellow believer to account.

then to make the picture more accurate still, there are other people taking part, and each one creates a set of ripples—which run into each other and affect each other.

Our mental and spiritual engagement with one another and the Lord doesn't alter the fundamentals of what's happening in any particular Lord's Supper. But, our interaction with one another can enhance the effect of the Lord's Supper on ourselves corporately and each of us individually.

The Lord's Supper is a transaction—a partnership—a sharing—a communi*cation*—with the Lord. Because it's an action, we should expect to be changed and affected. Something is being imparted to us. This action is a channel of grace in which God gives us desire and ability and understanding that go beyond our normal fleshly capabilities.

WHAT DOES "PARTICIPATION" MEAN?

Edward Calamy said more about how a believer participates in the Lord's Supper:

> [C]onsider the Mutual Action in this Ordinance, of *Giving* and *Taking,* between God and us, and you'll see plain Evidence in the Nature of the Thing, of a Covenant Transaction. *Giving* and *Taking* are the first obvious Actions in this Solemnity: *Giving* is God's part, and *Taking* ours. . . . As certainly as Bread and Wine is put into the Devout Communicant's Hands, so certainly is he invested in all Gospel-Privileges; so certainly hath he made over and conveyed to him, all Gospel-Benefits. God *Gives* Himself, his Son, his Spirit, his Grace, his Favor, and all that can be reasonably desired, or truly wanted, to the Believing Soul: This is on the one side. On the other side, the Believer *Takes*; Takes with his Hands the distributed Bread and Wine; and receives with all his Heart what is thereby Figured and Represented. He receives an offered Christ in his Arms and into his Heart; in short, God actually makes over, makes a Delivery, as it were, of all that he promises in the Covenant of Grace; on his part: We by *Taking* then what he *Gives*, do naturally engage to all that in that Covenant he hath made our Duty.[16]

A Christian leader from India, who wrote several centuries later, A. J. Appasamy, describes our "participation" in the body and blood of Christ another way. He says:

> Behold, the living Christ enters into us and forms a part of our inmost self in the same organic way in which food and drink become a part of our being. . . . Christ Himself comes into our souls through the elements and abiding in us endows us with His spiritual energy.

---

16   Calamy, *A Practical Discourse Concerning Vows*, 97–99.

Through faith we abide in Him.[17]

Here's the longest discussion on "participation" and the Lord's Supper in the Bible:

> So, my dear friends, flee from the worship of idols. You are reasonable people. Decide for yourselves if what I am saying is true. When we bless the cup at the Lord's Table, aren't we sharing in the blood of Christ? And when we break the bread, aren't we sharing in the body of Christ? And though we are many, we all eat from one loaf of bread, showing that we are one body. Think about the people of Israel. Weren't they united by eating the sacrifices at the altar?
>
> What am I trying to say? Am I saying that food offered to idols has some significance, or that idols are real gods? No, not at all. I am saying that these sacrifices are offered to demons, not to God. And I don't want you to participate with demons. You cannot drink from the cup of the Lord and from the cup of demons, too. You cannot eat at the Lord's Table and at the table of demons, too. What? Do we dare to rouse the Lord's jealousy? Do you think we are stronger than He is?[18]

Demonization is a reality—there are symptoms and effects which show up in an individual's behavior. (Of course, this reality isn't seen by people who start from a mindset that doesn't allow room for a spiritual realm. But demonization is certainly the simplest and most complete explanation of extreme evil and mental bizarreness.) Idol worship, in whatever form, opens a person to demonic influence, to being demonized. Can we see the sharing involved in the Lord's Supper as being the opposite— we are being "Christ-ized" instead of "demonized"!

---

17   A. J. Appasamy, *Christianity as Bhakti Marga: A Study of the Johannine Doctrine of Love* (Chennai, India: Christian Literature Society, 1928), 142, 147; quoted in Robin Boyd, *An Introduction to Indian Christian Theology,* (Delhi, India: Indian Society for Promoting Christian Knowledge, 1969), 139.

18   1 Corinthians 10:14–22, NLT.

CHAPTER 2

DOES COMMUNION REALLY MATTER?

Given the reality of participating with Christ,
communion is of the highest priority!

"AND THEY DEVOTED themselves to the apostles' teaching and the fellowship, to the breaking of bread and the prayers."[19] This short description of the life of the first believers highlights the importance of the Lord's Supper. It's meant to be a central part of our Christian life.

Nevertheless, over the years, the church at large appears to have let it slip in priority. Can we even relate to the following story?

> One Sabbath [Sunday] morning, during the reign of James II of England, as a captain with a party of soldiers went out to hunt down Protestants, as they termed it, they met a young woman, a servant-maid, running along the road early in the morning, without either shoes or stockings. The captain of the band asked her where she was going so early in the morning, and what was the urgency of the business that made her run so fast. She told him that she had learned her elder brother was dead, and she was going to receive her share of the riches he had bequeathed to her, as well as to her other

---

19 Acts 2:42, ESV. See Appendix 5 for a discussion of this passage.

brothers and sisters, and she was afraid she would be too late. The commander was so well pleased with her answer, that he gave her half-a-crown to buy a pair of shoes, and also wished her success; but if he had known the real business she was going on, which was to a sacrament, he would most probably have prevented her from going that day to the place where she hoped to receive "durable riches."[20]

Can we imagine that someone would risk life and limb simply to take part in the Lord's Supper? Or again, here's a story of the priority of the Lord's Supper for a recent convert:

One of the converted Greenlanders, who had taken a seal, rather than be absent from the missionary settlement when the Lord's Supper was to be administered, rowed the whole night in his kayak with the animal in tow, and when his exertion was mentioned—"How could I," said he, "stay where I was? My soul hungers and thirsts after the Lord and His communion."[21]

Richard Wurmbrand tells of someone who gave the Lord's Supper similar priority:

The secret police had come to search the house of Antonii, the Orthodox bishop of Arkhangelsk [in the Soviet Union]. Finding the vessel used for Holy Communion, they threw it on the floor and trampled on it. The bishop threw himself across it, trying to protect it

---

20 John Whitecross, *The Shorter Catechism Illustrated* (London: The Banner of Truth Trust, 1968 reprint of 1828 original), 151.
21 Ibid.

with his body. He lost consciousness. When he awoke,
he was in jail.[22]

One source of my mistaken priorities was in mistaken theology. I was, like many perhaps, really vague on how "God's acceptance of me by grace" and "my obedience" worked together. I didn't see the Lord's Supper as important because I didn't see Jesus' commands as important! Would I have said that in so many words? No, of course not. My focus has only recently become fixed on the simplicity of how we're to live, summed up in what's normally called the Great Commission. Here's a translation of that passage, using everyday English:

Then Jesus came to them and said, "All power in heaven
and on earth is given to me. So go and make followers
of all people in the world. Baptize them in the name of
the Father and the Son and the Holy Spirit. Teach them
to obey everything that I have taught you, and I will be
with you always, even until the end of this age."[23]

---

22 Wurmbrand, Richard, *The Sweetest Song* (London: Marshall Pickering, 1988), 99–100. Wurmbrand goes on to describe what happened to the bishop: They asked his opinion about the future of the Russian Church, and wanted to know if he desired the overthrow of the Soviets. He answered that the Church would be glorified through the suffering of its martyrs, as it was in the first centuries, and that he prayed daily that the Soviet government would not shed blood and would be forgiven for its sins.
First he was threatened with death, then was promised freedom if he would become an informer for the police. The bishop was not frightened, and could not be bought. He was put in a small cell together with five others. They endured bitter cold, and received only two glasses of water a day and nothing else. They could not wash or change their clothes, and lived in their own stench. They lost their teeth. The bishop became so weak that he could not clean the invading bugs and lice out of his beard. When he felt death near he chanted his own funeral service. He died with prayers on his lips. He was an authentic bride of Christ.

23 Matthew 28:18–19a, NCV.

Why do I say, "normally called the Great Commission"? Because this label may lead us to see it as a "task," one of a number of things in our lives "to be done." Instead, we need to see living this way as all about friendship with Jesus. It's "the Great Friendship" as well as "the Great Commission." It's a matter of "living with Him on His mission," because He said, "I am with you always" in the midst of our obedience.

We're to teach "all that" Jesus commanded in a way that results in others' obedience. This presumes our own obedience! This is a two-part calling, a two-part relationship: making followers, and teaching to obey. (Baptizing isn't a third part of the calling, but simply a first step of obedience.)

Make followers. Teach them to obey everything Jesus taught.

Based on that, mission statesman George Patterson trains cross-cultural church planters to focus on seven key commands of Jesus:[24]

- Repent and believe.[25]
- Be baptized and continue in the new life it initiates.[26]
- Love God and neighbor in a practical way.[27]
- Celebrate the Lord's Supper.[28]
- Pray.[29]
- Give.[30]
- Disciple others.[31]

We can argue whether his summary covers "everything" that Jesus taught, but it's more useful to actually begin emulating Patterson's

---

24   George Patterson, "The Spontaneous Multiplication of Churches" in *Perspectives of the World Christian Movement Reader,* eds. Ralph D. Winter and Steve Hawthorne (Pasadena, California: William Carey Library, 2009), 639.
25   Mark 1:15.
26   Matthew 28:18–20; Acts 2:38; Romans 6:1–11.
27   Matthew 22:37–40.
28   Luke 22:17–20.
29   Matthew 6:5–15.
30   Matthew 6:19–21; Luke 6:38.
31   Matthew 28:18–20.

advice! The key point for us to consider is that out of 382 imperatives (commands) given by Jesus in the New Testament, Patterson sees the command "Do this in remembrance of me" as one of the most important.[32] Do we?

Strikingly, the common thread in Patterson's short list is relationship. Patterson focuses on the principles needed to live in a dynamic relationship. He doesn't go into the details. That's what some of the commands in the Sermon on the Mount do as they direct us, for example, "Come to terms quickly with your accuser while you are going with him to court."[33] The details take care of themselves as we obey the really "big" commands—including the command to "Do this in remembrance of me."

The importance of the Lord's Supper isn't determined by my experience of it—but rather our Lord's valuation of it. God's view of our action is the measurement of its importance!

---

32   Peter Wittstock, *Hear Him! The One Hundred and Twenty-five Commands of Jesus* (Longwood, Florida: Xulon Press, 2004) Since Jesus is quoted as saying the same command in different gospels, Wittstock covers 224 of those imperatives in his 125 commands. He excluded the remaining 158 as being of little ongoing relevance because they were limited to the immediate situation (for instance, when Jesus commanded the woman at the well in Samaria to return to the well with her husband; John 4:16b).

33   Matthew 5:25, ESV.

DESIRE^2 (TO THE 2ND POWER)

The importance of the Last Supper to our Lord Jesus can't be minimized.

"Desire squared" is how you could describe the way Jesus described His intense longing to join His close friends in what we now call "The Last Supper." The King James Version reflects the Greek wording, but it's expressed awkwardly in English, "With desire I have desired to eat this passover with you before I suffer:"[34] Jesus used both the noun and the verb for desire. (The word is translated "lust" in other contexts.) He went on to say: "For I tell you that from now on I will not drink of the fruit of the vine until the kingdom of God comes."[35] Luke later described how on the day He rose again Jesus broke bread with two disciples in Emmaus, and vanished! Then he ate with the ten (Thomas was missing) that night.[36] John described Jesus preparing fish and bread for his disciples before his talk with Peter.[37]

Luke quotes Peter as describing eating and drinking as part of the evidence for Jesus' resurrection:

> And we are witnesses of all that he did both in the country of the Jews and in Jerusalem. They put him

---

34   Luke 22:15, KJV.
35   Luke 22:18, ESV.
36   Luke 24:28–48.
37   John 21:13.

to death by hanging him on a tree, but God raised him on the third day and made him to appear, not to all the people but to us who had been chosen by God as witnesses, who ate and drank with him after he rose from the dead.[38]

Jesus' statement that He wouldn't drink of the fruit of the vine "until the kingdom of God shall come" is helpful in our understanding of what makes up the presence of the kingdom of God. Perhaps someone might argue that Jesus hasn't drunk of the fruit of the vine yet; but it's difficult to imagine him eating without drinking, and drinking a normal drink of the time, wine. And Peter's specific words that they drank with Him, after He rose from the dead, point to the fulfillment of Jesus' even more specific prediction in Matthew, "I tell you I will not drink again of this fruit of the vine until that day when I drink it new with you in My Father's kingdom."[39]

Jesus drank with his followers here—in His Father's Kingdom. The Kingdom is present and the Lord's Supper is a Kingdom meal. Is the Kingdom complete yet? No—God's rule will be complete when He vanquishes every foe, including death and Hades.

---

38   Acts 10:39–41, ESV.
39   Matthew 26:29, ESV.

CHAPTER 3

COULD COMMUNION BE A MEAL?

THE MEANING OF "breaking of bread" in Acts 2:42 is important. Luke, the author of Acts, uses the term at the end of his gospel to describe a regular meal, after a long walk to Emmaus.[40] This meal occurred just six weeks before Acts 2:42. It's unlikely Luke would mean something different the next time he uses the term. Since Luke and Acts are a connected narrative, only 101 verses separate the two occurrences.

Four verses after Acts 2:42, Luke uses the original root of the word to describe eating together, "So continuing daily with one accord in the temple, and breaking bread from house to house, they [the first groups of Jesus followers] ate their food with gladness and simplicity of heart."[41] Here Luke is apparently referring to both a regular meal and the remembrance of the Lord. In John 6, Jesus told the crowd following Him that eating and drinking Him is essential. We can debate if He meant the Lord's Supper,[42] but we know the early church devoted themselves to three things: learning about the Lord and His ways (the apostles' teaching), partnership with one another and Jesus through prayer, and eating together. Here's a historical summary from a standard work on the Lord's Supper:

---

40   "And they told about the things that had happened on the road, and how He was known to them in the breaking of bread" (Luke 24:35, NKJV).

41   Acts 2:46, NKJV.

42   See the *Afterthought* for a discussion of John 6.

During the second century the church meal and strictly sacramental part of the meal were separated from one another and became two distinct occasions, and eventually the church meal or Agape fell into disuse. What is important is that right through the New Testament period and beyond Christians met together to hold common meals that were more than a token reception of bread and wine.[43]

Is it possible that in these short lines, we have a clue to what the Lord's Supper could become again? Even the writer's casual use of the phrase "token reception of bread and wine" points out the dramatic change from then to now. The word "token" highlights how our current approach changes, and diminishes, this remembrance of our Lord, compared to the practice of early believers.

For some Christ-followers, the practice of churches throughout history carries as much weight as the words of Scripture. Traditions are seen as the basis for how we should live out our faith. Whether or not that's so (Protestants maintain the Bible's directions are to be honored above traditions established later), wouldn't it be best to follow the earliest traditions in sharing the bread and the cup?

Looking at the practice of the early church gives a context to the words of Scripture. Seen together, the inevitable question is: What happened?

Was our Lord refining the conduct of church life as time progressed? Or was it the beginning of the institutionalization of the church at large? Was a living faith being turned into rote ceremonies, causing many people to go through the motions, without being engaged in their hearts?

I'm obviously using "institutionalization" in a negative way. What do I mean?

---

43   I. Howard Marshall, *Last Supper Lord's Supper* (Vancouver, Canada: Regent College Publishing, 1980), 111.

"Institutionalization" is where a structure, a framework of doing something, becomes more important than its original purpose and effect. As time went on, it's like the objects—the bread and the cup—became more important than the purpose of sharing the objects—namely, recognizing the special presence of Jesus in the midst of a united body of believers.

Much of the church became institutionalized when the Roman Emperor Constantine officially recognized Christianity, and then when Emperor Theodosion made it the state religion. Centuries later, but a century before the Reformation would begin, Peter Chelčický tied the corruption of the church structure in his day directly to the Roman Empire's actions. "When Emperor Constantine in his heathen mode of existence was taken up into the Church by Pope Sylvester and the latter in turn was fitted out with external power—it was then that the destruction of the Church was inevitable."[44] When we look back at history, it appears our Lord allowed a detour away from His purposes when He allowed a church structure to have earthly political power.

Is it possible that vibrant "love feasts," with both spontaneous human fellowship and the concentrated presence of our Lord, would have helped protect the church from the seductive temptation of earthly power? It's easy for history to focus on a dramatic event like Emperor Constantine's declaration of toleration. But is it possible that the gradual, undramatic institutionalization of the Lord's Supper could have been just as significant a step backward for the church?

Although the Supper's institutionalization occurred prior to the church becoming an ally of the civil government, certainly the change in the Supper went hand-in-hand with church leadership becoming an ongoing hierarchy. The Supper moved from being something anyone could lead to something reserved for only specially ordained people. Eventually, after Constantine's declaration of toleration, and then

---

44   Leonard Verduin, *The Reformers and Their Stepchildren* (Sarasota, Florida: Church Hymnary Publishers, 1991; reprint of 1964 original), 70.

Theodosion's establishment of Christianity as the state religion of the Roman Empire, church hierarchies became enmeshed with civil government and earthly power. By 385 AD, this had reached the point where a couple of bishops, instead of handling problems inside the church, went to the emperor's government to have another bishop, Priscillian of Avila, executed for teaching what they saw as wrong beliefs![45]

The phrase "thin edge of the wedge" describes how something seemingly insignificant can lead to changes and then to even bigger changes. The changes in the way the Lord's Supper was celebrated were part of the calcification of the church—and may have been the thin edge of the wedge! At a minimum, we need to restore the simple celebration of the Lord's Supper among all believers without rules requiring someone from a hierarchy to be present or requiring a particular formula. We don't want our obedience to be limited by secularly inspired traditions and the feelings associated with those traditions.[46]

---

45   Henry Chadwick, *Priscillian of Avila* (Cambridge: University of Cambridge Press, 1976).

46   For discussion of having the bread and the cup as part of a fuller meal, see Appendix 2.

CHAPTER 4

SYMBOLS REVEAL TRUTHS
TO OUR HEARTS

WHAT DOES BLOOD IMPLY? We see blood because of a wound—it doesn't come from pneumonia or old age. Nowadays we can see blood in a tube, as we donate after being poked by a comparatively painless needle. We might see the cup during the Lord's Supper as something similar—but we need remember that this blood comes from a violent sacrifice.

In John 6, we learn how Jesus offended people who were following Him so long as it seemed the "in" thing to do. In part, He offended them by forecasting His own violent sacrifice.[47] That sacrifice would continue to be an offense to Jews looking for God to come "in power," as a Messiah who would throw off the Roman oppression.[48]

"Blood" communicated something else to any Jew trained in the Torah. When Jesus said, "Drink my blood!" He was saying He would make atonement. "It is the blood that makes atonement."[49] By commanding people to drink His blood, our Lord was saying that He was

---

47   See the *Afterthought* for a further discussion of John 6.
48   "Has not God made foolish the wisdom of the world? For since, in the wisdom
      of God, the world did not know God through wisdom, it pleased God through
      the folly of what we preach to save those who believe. For Jews demand signs and
      Greeks seek wisdom, but we preach Christ crucified, a stumbling block to Jews
      and folly to Gentiles, but to those who are called, both Jews and Greeks, Christ
      the power of God and the wisdom of God" (1 Corinthians 1:17–24, ESV).
49   Leviticus 17:11b, ESV.

giving His blood as an atonement for them. Many Jews were outraged: "How could any human do that?"

What is atonement? One easy way to get its meaning is to break the English word into three parts different from its syllable division, "at-one-ment." It's the state of being brought together with God, being at one with Him.

The outrage at Jesus' radical instructions points to our blessing. There could and can be no part-time or half-way followers. Those who claim Jesus are incorporated into Him—and He into them—completely. We are the seed that dies to self, and becomes new life. Communion can reveal these truths to our heart. Verlon Fosner notes:

> Jesus focused His disciples solely on His death for a reason. There is something powerful in this isolated theme and its effect on evangelism. Paul highlights this in Romans 6, "we unite with him in his death." It's being united with Christ in His death that grips humankind. . . . The Great Commission and communion are saying the same thing. Focus on the death! Focus on the death!! Focus on the death!!! Something grand happens in a seeker when we focus them on Christ's death and our "death to self" in response to His. There are many things to live for, but what in this life is important enough to die for? That is the question beneath the question. There is profound mystery there! Deep talks to deep there! Christ reveals Himself there![50]

The fact that Jesus didn't try to make a formula out of what He said means we're left with mystery. We can be scandalized too, just like they were when Jesus was preaching to them in the flesh. After all, how can we teach about the God of the universe's grand plan for humans through the

---

50   Verlon Fosner, *The Sacred Invite*, unpublished paper, January 2008, 19–20. Used with permission. Fosner suggests communion is "the sacred invite" and can be a "jack hammer of revelation."

simple act of sharing bread and a drink? Or we can reflect, in awe, on the victory and mercy which were combined when He came to earth and gave up His life for our sakes.

If you've read this far, you may be familiar with lists of "Who We Are in Christ." For instance, here's a list I've carried with me, reminding me that I am:

- A child of God — 1 John 3:1–2
- In Christ — 1 Corinthians 1:30
- Christ's friend — John 15:15
- A slave of God — Romans 6:22
- An heir of God — Galatians 4:6–7
- Joint heir with Christ — Romans 8:17
- A temple of God — 1 Corinthians 3:16
- Indwelled by God's Spirit — 1 Corinthians 6:19
- A member of Christ's body — 1 Corinthians 12:27
- Reconciled to God — 2 Corinthians 5:18–19
- God's workmanship — Ephesians 2:10
- Hidden with Christ in God — Colossians 3:3
- Chosen of God — Ephesians 1:4
- Dearly loved — Ephesians 1:4

The above is only half of this particular list—and there are others. But how real are these truths, in our experience? The times the list "feels" true in our experience may be rare, unfortunately. Certainly, I often don't "live" much of the list. But there are those times we do live them—when we've been loving others, expressing devotion to God in prayer and music, or simply accepting the tasks of life cheerfully because we catch sight of the joy He has over us and has available for us.

Is it possible that our list of who we are in Christ can become a deeper experience in our lives when we develop the intimacy which is available in Christ through sharing the bread and the cup with others? Every occasion of the Lord's Supper opens a channel of impartation—conveying new heart knowledge from God to us—making more real who we are in Christ!

MORE THAN ARBITRARY

Let's look at aspects of the Lord's Supper as they appear
throughout the Bible.

A symbiosis
A synergy
A symmetry
A synthesis
Of symbols.

"Melchizedek, king of Salem, brought out bread and wine."[a]

"I am the bread of life."[b]
"And he took bread . . . this is my body."[c]
"The Lord Jesus . . . took bread, and when he had given thanks He broke it."[d]

"They are to eat the lamb, together with unleavened bread . . .
they must not . . . break any of its bones."[e]
"When they came to Jesus and saw he was already dead,
they did not break His legs."[f]
"The Lord . . . protects all his bones, not one of them will be broken."[g]

"The blood is the life."[h]
"Whoever . . . drinks my blood has eternal life."[i]
"Is not the cup of thanksgiving for which we give thanks
a participation in the blood of Christ?"[j]

" I will not drink wine again until the day I drink it new with you
in my Father's Kingdom."[k]
"Everyone brings out the choice wine first. . .
but you have saved the best till now."[l]
"The LORD Almighty will prepare . . . the finest of wines. . . .
He will swallow up death forever."[m]

"It is the blood that makes atonement for one's life."[n]
"This cup is the new 'last will and testament' in My blood."[o]

———————————

a   Genesis 14:18, ESV.
b   John 6:48, ESV.
c   Luke 22:19, ESV.
d   1 Corinthians, 11:23–24, ESV.
e   Numbers 9:11–12, NIV.
f   John 19:33, ESV.
g   Psalm 34:20, NIV.
h   Deuteronomy 12:23, ESV.
i   John 6:54, ESV.
j   1 Corinthians 10:16a, NIV.
k   Matthew 26:29, NLT.
l   John 2:10, NIV.
m   Isaiah 25:6, 8a, NIV.
n   Leviticus 17:11, NIV.
o   1 Corinthians 11:25, *God's Word to the Nations—New Evangelical Transla-tion—New Testament,* (Cleveland: NET Publishing, 1990) 319.

BLOOD ESTABLISHES GOD'S LAST WILL AND TESTAMENT

The cup of wine is tied to an action—a violent and sacrificial death accomplished by our Lord—as He gave up His life at the hands of sinners. The wine isn't simply representing a substance, but an action. No matter how committed one human is to another, a victim of a disease can't be said to have "poured out his blood" for a friend.

Abram's initial covenant with Yahweh (before Abram's name change) was confirmed with the death, the sacrifice, of animals. His further covenant was confirmed with circumcision, which involves blood.

Moses' leadership of the escape from Egypt began with blood; the Passover lamb was killed and blood put on the doorposts. After the Exodus from Egypt, God made a new commitment, or covenant, with the Hebrew people. It was confirmed with blood:

> Then he [Moses] sent some of the young Israelite men to present burnt offerings and to sacrifice bulls as peace offerings to the LORD. Moses drained half the blood from these animals into basins. The other half he splattered against the altar. Then he took the Book of the Covenant and read it aloud to the people. Again they all responded, "We will do everything the LORD has commanded. We will obey." Then Moses took the blood from the basins and splattered it over the people, declaring, "Look, this blood confirms the covenant the LORD has made with you in giving you these instructions."[51]

Interestingly, the leaders of the Hebrew people then ate a meal before the Lord:

> Then Moses, Aaron, Nadab, Abihu, and the seventy elders of Israel climbed up the mountain. There they saw the God of Israel. Under his feet there seemed

---

51 Exodus 24:5–8, NLT.

to be a surface of brilliant blue lapis lazuli, as clear as the sky itself. And though these nobles of Israel gazed upon God, he did not destroy them. In fact, they ate a covenant meal, eating and drinking in his presence![52]

Covenants in the Old Testament were promises of things to come. When Jesus said, "This cup is the new testament in my blood" (as the King James Version translates[53],) there was a subtle but critical difference. Once a person dies, a last will and testament becomes an accomplished legal fact—the directions contained in the document need to be carried out. The phrase "last will and testament" does clarify what's happening in the Lord's Supper particularly because "covenant" is currently used in several different ways. Those familiar with the Bible will use "covenant" in that context. Someone else might refer to "the covenant of marriage" but most other contemporary use is for mundane legal restrictions on real estate in a mutually agreed-upon contract. That kind of meaning makes the word "covenant" scarcely suitable to convey the great truth of God's commitment to us. The words "last will and testament" emphasize that we can add nothing to Jesus' finished work, His sacrifice. Our role is simply to accept our inheritance.

Martin Luther said, "For if God is to make a testament, as He promises, then He must die; and if He is to die, then He must be a man. And so that little word 'testament' is a short summary of all God's wonders and grace, fulfilled in Christ."[54]

The translators of the New Evangelical Translation of the New Testament illustrate this point further, looking at the most well-known passage in the Bible, John 3:16:

> John 3:16: "For God [the Testator] loved the world [the heirs] so much that He gave [into death]

---

52 Exodus 24:9–11, NLT.
53 1 Corinthians 11:25 and parallels: Matthew 26:28; Mark 14:24; and Luke 22:20.
54 God's Word to the Nations—New Evangelical Translation—New Testament, (Cleveland: NET Publishing, 1990), 539; quoting Luther's Works (Philadelphia: Muhlenberg Press, 1960), XXXV, 84f.

His unique Son, so that everyone who believes in Him would not perish [the Testator's signature by word of promise] but have everlasting life [the inheritance]. . . . Isn't it interesting that this passage just happens to be in "testamental" form? When a person goes to an attorney to draw up his "last will and testament," five things are usually involved: (1) *a testator,* the one who makes up the will; (2) *heir(s);* (3) *a method of effectuation,* the way by which a testament goes into effect (by death); (4) *a testator's promissory signature,* which validates—through his word of promise—that which will be given to the heir(s; and (5) *the actual inheritance* to be left behind.[55]

Before we leave this subject, let's remember the unique character of this particular "last will and testament." Here's a passage where Isaiah prophesied about the Savior to come— and declared that the Savior Himself will be our covenant, or testament: "I am the LORD; I have called you in righteousness; I will take you by the hand and keep you; I will give you as a covenant for the people, a light for the nations."[56]

Our covenant, our last will and testament, is a person! We meet Him afresh through His Supper.

---

55 Ibid.
56 Isaiah 42:6, ESV.

CHAPTER 5

SOMBER SUPPER OR JOYFUL PARTY?

IS OUR VIEW of God too limited and predictable? C. S. Lewis' representation of Jesus in the character Aslan is well known—Mr. Beaver makes the key observation to the children in the *The Lion, The Witch and The Wardrobe*: "He's wild, you know. Not like a tame lion." I would say tame ceremonies can't express the reality of a wild God! Measured against the tone of Scripture, many current occasions of the Lord's Supper feel like a real party has been replaced by a hollow shell.

My hope is that these comments will contribute to a "communion revival" to bring new vitality to our spiritual experience.

I implore us, as the body of Christ, to examine our hearts, minds, and mouths as we approach the Lord's Supper. Let's revise our practices to bring more life back to what often feels to me like a duty—not a privilege of a high and holy experience in the Lord.

Some churches I've been part of say we "celebrate"[57] the Lord's Supper, but can we honestly say any of these phrases describe our emotional experiences (emphases added)?

---

57   I use quotation marks around "celebrate" to draw attention to how we may casually use the term in describing an occasion of having the Lord's Supper, and yet the emotional intensity seems a long way from a graduation, a wedding, an awards ceremony or a victory party.

- the cup of *thanksgiving* for which we give thanks[58]
- a *participation* in the blood of Christ[59]
- [T]hey *devoted* themselves . . . to the fellowship, to the breaking of bread.[60]
- [E]very day . . . they broke bread in their homes and ate together with *glad* and *sincere* hearts, praising God.[61]
- On the first day of the week we came *together* to break bread. . . . Then he went upstairs again and *broke bread and ate*.[62]

Is the overall tone of the event really one of thanksgiving in us? Does it evoke expressions of joy and praise?

Is it a corporate experience, connecting us with each other and transcendent mystery, or is it only an instance of many isolated individual thoughts taking place in the same room?

Are we devoted to the breaking of bread as much as to preaching and prayer? Should we be?

Do we share the bread and the cup as we eat together in our potlucks or covered dish meals?

Is the reason we come together to experience the Lord's presence in His Supper?

Are we willing to devote a substantial amount of time at our gatherings to a meal and celebration of the Lord's Supper? Do we consume the Lord's Supper quicker than a school lunch? Is it possible we're uncomfortable with time spent in silence and contemplation? Do we lack the spiritual stamina to keep focusing on the Lord Jesus for more than a moment?

A number of times we're commanded to be joyful but from what I see of the church (at least in the developed world), this may be God's least

---

58 1 Corinthians 10:16a, NIV.
59 1 Corinthians 10:16b, NIV.
60 Acts 2:42, ESV.
61 Acts 2:46–47a, NIV.
62 Acts 20:7, 11, NIV.

obeyed direction![63] My observations of nearly all people taking part in a Lord's Supper would give me no evidence they're experiencing joy.

So, if our emotions don't match the New Testament experience, is it possible this may be due to two factors: lack of expectancy and lack of obedience? Let's allow those questions to ferment, and trust for excellent wine to be brought forth.

Lest one think that I'm suggesting something I'm not, allow me to quote C. S. Lewis to convey something of what I am longing for:

> [I]t is immortals whom we joke with, work with, marry, snub, and exploit—immortal horrors or everlasting splendors. This does not mean we are to be perpetually solemn. We must play. But our merriment must be of that kind (and it is, in fact, the merriest kind) which exists between people who have, from the outset, taken each other seriously—no flippancy, no superiority, no presumption. And our charity must be a real and costly love, with deep feeling for the sins in spite of which we love the sinner—no mere tolerance or indulgence which parodies love as flippancy parodies merriment.[64]

How can we move forward? How can we respond more fully to the Lord's commands? I don't have a complete answer. I trust we can learn principles from the corrections I describe in these pages of my past mistakes. The appendices include specific scripts and suggestions, particularly

---

63   "Finally, my brothers, rejoice in the Lord. . . . Rejoice in the Lord always; again I will say, Rejoice" (Philippians 3:1a, 4:4, ESV) is a most telling example of such a command. Another instruction, spoken at the close of Jesus' earthly ministry is equally compelling: "These things I have spoken to you, that my joy may be in you, and that your joy may be full" (John 15:11, ESV). For a fuller exploration of this theme, see *Champagne for the Soul* by Mike Mason.

64   C. S. Lewis, *The Weight of Glory* (New York: Harper Collins, 2000; reprint of 1949 original), 46.

in Appendix 3. One way forward is to consciously recognize Jesus' presence at a meal with friends, by sharing the bread and the cup.

Another route forward would be to change the size of our celebration. Passover meals always have a practical limitation—one lamb can only feed so many people. At the same time, you need several people to eat a whole lamb. Josephus, in *The Jewish Wars,* describes the Passover circa 70 AD: "as it is not possible to feast alone a sort of fraternal group is formed around each victim [the lamb], consisting of at least ten adult males, while many groups have twenty members."[65] I realize, in terms of our meal, we have a lamb who is infinite and capable of feeding the entire human race at one sitting. But, at the Last Supper, Jesus only included a small number of His followers. Wouldn't it enhance our enjoyment of our meal to have it at least as often in smaller groups as we celebrate it in a larger corporate worship service? Let's celebrate it in smaller "love circles"—like the circle of the twelve disciples.

Part of the route forward simply involves a conscious shift in our emotional expectancy in approaching communion. I can imagine the apostle Paul visiting one of our communion services and saying "Whoa! Let's get back to eating together with gladness and sincerity of heart. Just because my Corinthian friends went wild with their parties doesn't mean you shouldn't have a party in our Lord's presence!"

Communion helps us hold the paradox of "serious joy" in our hearts. In a similar way, the French scholar Jean Danielou has written on "sober inebriation" as a description of the wonder of communion. He has found this theme among a number of the early church fathers. One was Gregory of Nyssa:

> In giving it the wine that rejoices man's heart, Christ produces in the soul this sober inebriation which raises

---

65   Josephus, *The Jewish Wars,* trans. G. A. Williamson, revised ed. (London: Penguin Books, 1970), 379. William Whiston's translation doesn't specify "adult males" (public domain, Vol. 6,9,3).

the dispositions of the heart from passing things to what is eternal; "And my inebriating chalice, how wonderful it is [from the Septuagint translation of Psalm 23]."[66]

Danielou quotes Ambrose as saying in terms of communion:

This chalice has inebriated the nations, so that they no longer remember their own sadness and forget their ancient error. This is why this spiritual inebriation is good, not affecting our physical powers, but lifting up the soaring spirit; the inebriation of the chalice is good, for it does away with the sadness of a sinful conscience and pours out the joy of everlasting life. This is why Scripture says "And Thy inebriating chalice is wonderful."[67]

---

66   Jean Danielou. *The Bible and the Liturgy.* (Notre Dame, Indiana: University of Notre Dame Press, first paperback edition 1966.) 185.

67   Ibid. 184–185.

SHOULD FEELINGS GUIDE OUR PRACTICES?

A re emotions simply neutral? Are they beyond our soul's direction?

Emotions were affected by the Fall. Sin has damaged them, as well as impairing our thinking and social relations. And while emotions may seem to "just happen," they can be affected. Dallas Willard notes: "We can choose to take in the Word of God, and when we do that, feelings and beliefs will be steadily pulled in a godly direction."[68]

The church has spent much time focused on "orthodoxy"—that is, right knowing or thinking. Yet, as Willard and others will point out, right thinking isn't sufficient to bring about the fruit we should see from God's rule in our lives. Many decisions, no matter how we may justify them, are shaped ultimately by our feelings more than by our thoughts.

Church leaders at large need to model, teach toward, and focus on "orthopathy"—right passions. If "right passions" become our goal and guide, our decisions will go in new directions. We'll walk in new paths.

So when the Bible describes emotions that accompany particular things, such as the joy in heaven that accompanies someone's repentance, we can aim for our emotions to line up with that. When they don't, it's reasonable to ask, how come? What's missing?

Since "thanksgiving" and "gladness" accompany the Lord's Suppers described in the New Testament, we can aim for our practices to produce these, rather than boredom or condemnation focused on our unworthiness.

---

68 Dallas Willard, *Renovation of the Heart* (Colorado Springs: NavPress, 2002), 248.

CHAPTER 6

WHAT DOES BORED OBEDIENCE DO?

"THESE PEOPLE HONOR me with their lips, but their hearts are far from me. Their worship is a farce, for they teach man-made ideas as commands from God."[69]

Could these words describe a quick routine act of a small wafer and a teaspoon of grape juice in a tiny cup? Sure, obedience to Christ won't always be fun, seem meaningful, or produce obvious fruit in our lives. Yet, at some point, don't we run the danger that the dull repetition of an act becomes meaningless?

Why am I concerned? Because our Lord hates empty acts of worship! Jesus quoted Isaiah in the words above. Isaiah was describing meaningless worship in his day. Isaiah proclaims this at the beginning of his book as well:

> "The multitude of your sacrifices—what are they to me?" says the LORD. "I have more than enough of burnt offerings, of rams and the fat of fattened animals; I have no pleasure in the blood of bulls and lambs and goats. When you come to appear before me, who has asked this of you, this trampling of my courts? Stop bringing meaningless offerings!"[70]

---

69 Matthew 15:8, NLT.
70 Isaiah 1:11–13a, NIV.

Consider the prophet Malachi's stirring words along similar lines:

> A son honors his father,
> and a servant fears his master;
> If, then, I am a father,
> where is the honor due to me?
> And if I am a master,
> where is the fear due to me?
> So says the LORD of hosts to you, O priests,
> who disdain my name.
> But you ask, "How have we disdained your name?"
> By offering defiled food on my altar!
> You ask, "How have we defiled it?"
> By saying that the table of the LORD may be disdained!
>
> When you offer a blind animal for sacrifice,
> is there no wrong in that?
> When you offer a lame or sick animal,
> is there no wrong in that?
> Present it to your governor!
> Will he be pleased with you—or show you favor?
> says the LORD of hosts.
> So now implore God's favor, that he may have mercy on us!
> You are the ones who have done this;
> Will he show favor to any of you?
> says the LORD of hosts.
> Oh, that one of you would just shut the temple gates
> to keep you from kindling fire on my altar in vain!
> I take no pleasure in you, says the LORD of hosts;
> and I will not accept any offering from your hands![71]

---

71 Malachi 1:6–10, NABre.

God's passion about meaningless religious actions was given further voice when Jesus came. In the Sermon on the Mount he referred to those who aren't Jews: "When you pray, don't babble on and on as the Gentiles do. They think their prayers are answered merely by repeating their words again and again. Don't be like them."[72] Does the same ritual of communion repeated over and over again become alarmingly like these Gentile prayers?

But nearly all of Jesus' criticism of religious practices was reserved for some of his fellow Jews. He denounced, as hypocrisy, acts of devotion to God that were done with wrong hearts:

> What sorrow awaits you teachers of religious law and you Pharisees. Hypocrites! For you are so careful to clean the outside of the cup and the dish, but inside you are filthy—full of greed and self-indulgence! You blind Pharisee! First wash the inside of the cup and the dish, and then the outside will become clean, too.[73]

In their hearts, they were far from obedience to the Lord. Their hypocrisy was obvious to Jesus, and no doubt to others.

Sure, the term "hypocrites" describes those who claim to follow Jesus but don't show by their behavior that they're obeying His commands. But what about those who obey one of His commands, like the Lord's Supper—but don't engage their hearts?

That kind of hypocrisy is less visible. After all, "the Lord sees not as man sees: man looks on the outward appearance, but the Lord looks on the heart."[74] Our heart attitudes can be hidden. Still Jesus said there is a way to look at a person's heart: "For out of the abundance of the heart the

---

72 Matthew 6:7–8a, NLT.
73 Matthew 23:25–26, NLT.
74 1 Samuel 16:7b, ESV.

mouth speaks."[75] We may be able to tell that someone else is just "going through the motions."

If leaders are concerned that people are just going through the motions, we should ask: "Have we contributed to their hypocrisy?" Leaders share responsibility for how a group responds to our Lord. The man I call my spiritual grandfather, Jim Wilson, had a sense of that responsibility. He told me about asking a child if he'd enjoyed an adult meeting, and then regretting the question the moment the words came out of his mouth—because Jim knew he was tempting the child to lie and say he did enjoy what was for him a boring time!

This applies to communion services as well—we can tempt people to "go through the motions" if we give little thought or preparation to how we celebrate the Lord's Supper. We want to do the reverse. We want to see people engaged in an authentic way with our Lord, participating in His promises. We have a responsibility to draw people's feelings, as well as their thoughts, Godward.

---

75 Matthew 12:34b, ESV.

THE PARABLE OF A MOM'S DYING WISH

Their mother was dying, but in that state of heightened alertness that sometimes just precedes physical death. All four sons were there, all young men now, and she motioned for them to come close, as her voice was still quiet: "Now boys, what would mean more to me than a granite headstone or anything like that, is that you would agree to gather together and take a hike on Rockwell's Mount, each year on my birthday. You know how much that place has always meant to me, and the family times we had there?"

With that intensity of presence which come in such moments, she looked at each son in turn—and they each nodded. No words needed to be spoken—it was understood!

Year One: The sons had breakfast at a café, and then spent the morning hiking all the way around the mountain. There wasn't a lot said during the whole morning, but the silence was warm and spoke volumes.

Year Two: This time, there was a little more planning. Two of them were married by this time, and their wives prepared a picnic and joined them to cap off the morning with the meal. One wife actually got a stream of conversation going, "Remember when Mom. . . ."

Year Three: Sam had moved away from the area. He seemed so pressured by his work that in the time leading up to her birthday Dick had felt like he was pressuring him to come, "After all, you remember what we told Mom?" Sam did end up breaking away from his busy season and joined in on the hike after breakfast. He gulped down some of the picnic before driving back to put in a half-day.

Year Four: Two of the families now had babies, and the men brought them on the hike—but Sam absolutely begged off because of work commitments. Dick was beside himself: "What would I say to Mom?" he agonized to his wife. He didn't want to break relationship over a hike—but he wanted to honor their mother! "How come we don't see it the same?" he almost shouted to himself.

Year Five: Larry had an idea—"Sam, could you make it if we did an evening hike, so you could come after work and wouldn't have to take any time off?" The four brothers agreed to meet at 7 pm. Even though they needed flashlights for the last leg of the hike, they made it work! They had decided it wasn't really workable for their toddlers. "It's probably better if it's just us sons anyway! We were the ones she asked!"

Year Six: Daryl had now moved out of their hometown as well, so they agreed to meet at 7 again, and skip any meal just so they could have time for the hike before it got really dark.

Year Seven: That had worked so well, they simply did it again.

Year Eight: And again.

Year Nine: And again.

Year Ten: Larry suggested a shorter route, and they decided to make the time 7:30 to better accommodate the out-of-towners.

Year Eleven: That's what they did again.

Year Twelve: And again.

Year Thirteen: Dick wondered if it was really worth doing this year, with all the things going on. "No," said Sam, "it's what Mom wanted us to do. I've got an idea—what if we included our older children this year?"

Year Sixty: Some of the cousins continued to meet for an evening hike. "I think it has something to do with our dads' mom?"

CHAPTER 7

POWER FLOWS THROUGH THESE SYMBOLS

THE LORD'S SUPPER is rooted in the context of the Passover meal.[76] Let's look at the Exodus of the Hebrew slaves from Egypt, and see the power of Passover.

> On the tenth day of this month each man is to take a lamb for his family, one for each household. . . . That same night they are to eat the meat roasted over the fire, along with bitter herbs, and bread made without yeast. Do not eat the meat raw or boiled in water, but roast it over a fire—head, legs and internal organs. Do not leave any of it till morning; if some is left till morning, you must burn it. This is how you are to eat it: with your cloak tucked into your belt, your sandals on your feet and your staff in your hand. Eat it in haste, it is the Lord's Passover.
>
> "On that same night I will pass through Egypt and strike down every firstborn of both people and animals, and I will bring judgment on all the gods of

---

76   There's debate whether Jesus was having a preparatory meal or an actual Passover Feast. The following sidebar is a discussion of the question.

Egypt. I am the Lord. The blood will be a sign for you
on the houses where you are, and when I see the blood,
I will pass over you. No destructive plague will touch
you when I strike Egypt.[77]

Note: they are to eat *all* of the lamb. Now let's consider what that
meal fueled—the flight from Egypt.[78] We're told about that massive
escape, "He [the Lord] brought them forth also with silver and gold: and
there was not one feeble person among their tribes."[79] Bible commentator Matthew Henry says:

> Their lives had been made bitter to them, and their bod-
> ies and spirits broken by their bondage; and yet, when
> God brought them forth, there was not one feeble per-
> son, none sick, none so much as sickly, among their
> tribes. They went out that very night that the plague
> swept away all the first-born of Egypt, and yet they went
> out all in good health, and brought not with them any
> of the diseases of Egypt. Surely never was the like, that
> among so many thousands there was not one sick![80]

Another commentator explains that the phrase "there was not one
feeble person" means "literally, not one who was lame; or, who halted, or
staggered." This commentator does go on to add what sounds like skepticism, "This, of course, is not necessarily to be understood literally."[81] Yet

---

77   Exodus 12:3, 8–13, NIV.
78   My thanks to British Bible teacher Kevin Matthews, who was first person I heard
      make this connection for me.
79   Psalm 105:37, KJV.
80   Matthew Henry, *Matthew Henry's Commentary on the Whole Bible* [E-Sword
      computer software] (Franklin, Tennessee: Equipping Ministry Foundation, n.d.).
81   Albert Barnes, *Albert Barnes Notes on the Bible* [E-Sword computer software]
      (Franklin, Tennessee: Equipping Ministry Foundation, n.d.).

Matthew Henry's remarks seem more to the point—particularly if we consider the situation in the days leading up to the Exodus:

> Then the slave drivers and the foremen went out and said to the people, "This is what the Pharaoh says: 'I will not give you any more straw. Go and get your own straw wherever you can find it, but your work will not be reduced at all.'" . . . And Pharaoh's slave drivers beat the Israelite overseers they had appointed, demanding, "Why haven't you met your quota of bricks yesterday or today, as before?"[82]

If their workload was increased, if there were beatings, it's reasonable that in a population of that size there would be those who were lame, even crippled, as well as sick. But the word says there was "not one feeble" after eating the Passover.

May I suggest the power of the Passover and the power the Lord's Supper are linked and that healing both accompanies and is evidence of the special presence of God and His Kingdom rule? I would tie this event—the supernatural health of the Hebrew Exodus—together with this passage:

> For if you eat the bread or drink the cup without honoring the body of Christ, you are eating and drinking God's judgment upon yourself. That is why many of you are weak and sick and some have even died.[83]

Here, the power of the Lord's Supper is described in the negative—eating and drinking without recognizing the body of the Lord brings on

---

82   Exodus 5:10, 14, NIV.
83   1 Corinthians 11:28–29, NLT.

judgment which allows the normal course of the fallen creation to oper-
ate, complete with decay, disease, and physical death. [84]

I ask myself more than occasionally, as you may, how come not
everyone who's prayed for is healed? I know there's a place for recognizing the process of prayer, the meaning of suffering, the Spirit's free will
in distributing gifts, and human responses to His work. And of course,
I ask myself, "Is there also a need for a 'level' of faith?" As someone who
used to suffer from a chronic health problem, I've endured the burden of
thinking my lack of healing was because of my lack of faith![85]

But when I've heard others talk about the question of why aren't more
people healed, I've rarely heard Paul's clear statement referred to. He
describes why there weren't healings in a specific New Testament church:
a corporate failure on the part of the members to properly recognize the
body of the Lord in the context of eating and drinking together![86] Is this
corporate failure similar to the two occasions in Jesus' ministry when a
lack of corporate faith hinders healing? One occurred when the disciples
couldn't drive out a demonic spirit causing seizures in a boy. They asked
what was going on and Jesus said: "Because of your little faith.[87] The
other occasion was when Jesus couldn't do miracles in his hometown of
Nazareth. Yet even there, Mark does say: "And because of their unbelief,

---

84   Honoring, recognizing or discerning the body of Christ in the context of Paul's
      rebuke to the Corinthian church means, at a minimum, that wealthier believers
      should be aware of the needs of, and their bond with, poorer believers. Certainly
      the spiritual discernment of Jesus's body in the group and in the bread can be
      included in Paul's words, but given the reason for Paul's words, concern for the
      right treatment of those in financial need has to be primary.
85   I appreciated hearing Nicky Gumbel's perspective in the 2003 edition of *The
      Alpha Course, "Is Healing for Today?"* that while Jesus stated the positive: That
      an indvidual's faith was responsible for his or her healing (Matthew 15:28, Mark
      5:34, Mark 10:52, Luke 8:48, Luke 18:42); when Jesus said lack of faith had lim-
      ited God's activity, it was in terms of a group's lack of faith. This is when the dis-
      ciples were attempting to deliver a young boy from demonic oppression.
86   1 Corinthians 11:28–29.
87   Matthew 17:20a, NABre. "Your" is plural.

He couldn't do any miracles among them except to place His hands on a few sick people and heal them."[88]

So to view this from the positive perspective: When we do eat and drink while recognizing the body of the Lord as a group, we allow the free flow of the gifts of God for health and healing. This is consistent with the benefits of the first Passover meal.

Certainly "recognizing the body of the Lord" is in large part realizing that we who are well-off are one with those who are needy. Each believer is part of one body. Paul's passionate comments about the Lord's Supper in 1 Corinthians are because he's upset that affluent believers haven't waited for the needy and they haven't eaten the supper together. The application of this principle is even broader—on two levels.

First, this is a transaction, an interaction. We aren't going through a mental exercise; we're joining hands in partnership with the risen Lord. He really and truly is the head of the Body—not merely in a metaphorical sense, but in actuality. He's intimately connected with us.

Second, the action of doing this together is vital—and in that action recognizing that we are united with all the different, unique, and even incongruous members of the Body of Christ. This means the ones we like, those we don't like, or those we're indifferent to.

However, in another sense, recognizing the Body of the Lord is simply being aware of the gospel! The fact that Jesus has done it all, and we simply need to receive His free gifts—of mercy and salvation, of grace and righteousness, of access and purpose. At its most basic level, the Lord's Supper reminds us, in every sense, of the gospel of Jesus Christ, crucified and victorious.

So we come full circle. The Lord's Supper isn't just a mental exercise, but our engagement with it—our involvement in it, our attitude—is vital to "recognizing the body of the Lord." Our hearts appear to be the key in allowing either a flow of explosive power or inviting judgment through

---

88   Mark 6:5, NLT.

illness and poor health. Annie Dillard's wonderful word picture applies
to the Lord's Supper with particular force:

> Does anyone have the foggiest idea of what sort of
> power we so blithely invoke? Or, as I suspect, does no
> one believe a word of it? The churches are children play-
> ing on the floor with their chemistry sets, mixing up a
> batch of TNT to kill a Sunday morning. It is madness
> to wear ladies' straw hats and velvet hats to church; we
> should all be wearing crash helmets. Ushers should issue
> life preservers and signal flares; they should lash us to
> our pews.[89]

---

89   Annie Dillard, *Teaching a Stone to Talk: Expeditions and Encounters* (New York:
     Harper & Row, 1982), 40–41.

WAS THE LAST SUPPER A PASSOVER MEAL?

Matthew, Mark, and Luke say Jesus was looking forward to eating the Passover and that his disciples prepared a Passover meal.[90] But John refers to the day of Jesus' crucifixion as day of preparation which would mean the Passover was to be eaten after Jesus died on the cross.[91]

Some readers might even see this difference as evidence the Bible is unreliable (although I suspect such a reader would be approaching the gospels with a bias!) Can it be resolved?

Colin Humphreys does a masterful job of examining ancient calendars, astronomical records, and other evidence as he puts forward a convincing case that there were two Passover dates used in Jerusalem in AD 33.[92] Galileans (as well as some other people) arrived at one date, using a lunar calendar for their calculations, while the Jewish leaders held to a different date, using a different calendar. Thus John's words "the Passover of

---

90 And on the first day of Unleavened Bread, when they sacrificed the Passover lamb, his disciples said to him, "Where will you have us go and prepare for you to eat the Passover?" And he sent two of his disciples and said to them, "Go into the city, and a man carrying a jar of water will meet you. Follow him, and wherever he enters, say to the master of the house, 'The Teacher says, Where is my guest room, where I may eat the Passover with my disciples?' And he will show you a large upper room furnished and ready; there prepare for us." And the disciples set out and went to the city and found it just as he had told them, and they prepared the Passover (Mark 14:12–16, ESV). Similar passages are found in Matthew 26:17–19 and Luke 22:7–13.

91 So when Pilate heard these words, he brought Jesus out and sat down on the judgment seat at a place called The Stone Pavement, and in Aramaic Gabbatha. Now it was the day of Preparation of the Passover. It was about the sixth hour. He said to the Jews, "Behold your King!" (John 19:13–14, ESV). Since it was the day of Preparation, and so that the bodies would not remain on the cross on the Sabbath (for that Sabbath was a high day), the Jews asked Pilate that their legs might be broken and that they might be taken away (John 19:31, ESV).

92 Colin Humphreys, *The Mystery of the Last Supper* (London: Cambridge University Press, 2011), 151–164.

the Jews"[93] can be seen as subtly distinguishing the Passover he refers to throughout his account from the meal that Jesus had with his disciples. From Humphreys' evidence, the Last Supper and Jesus' arrest took place on what would be Wednesday night in our calendar. Humphreys' understanding allows more time—all of Thursday and then Friday morning—for the various trials and back-and-forth maneuvers involved in deciding on Jesus' crucifixion.

---

93 Now the Passover of the Jews was at hand, and many went up from the country to Jerusalem before the Passover to purify themselves (John 11:55, ESV).

PARALLEL LINES

Without beginning or end
The King of Righteousness, King of Peace
Met Abraham and brought out—bread and wine.

The beginning and the end—
The King who makes us righteous, brings peace
Meets with sons of Abraham in bread and wine.

The leader of the deliverance prayed
And bread from heaven, manna,
Came down for the Hebrews to eat
And they ate and were hungry again.

And He, the deliverer, prayed and as
The bread from heaven went about earth
He came down that we could eat
And not be hungry again.

No lamb's bone would be broken
No yeast in the bread.

And He, the deliverer, prayed and as
His body given, but not a bone broken
No sin in His body.

The intermediary confirmed a new way
God would relate to His people

By sprinkling blood on them.
He announced that
The life is in the blood.

And He, the deliverer, prayed
And as the mediator
Confirmed a new way
God would relate to His people
With a cup of thanksgiving.
Whoever drinks His blood
Has eternal life.

CHAPTER 8

INCREASING EXPECTANCY

OUR EXPECTANCY ABOUT the effects of the Lord's Supper may be limited by our experience. Let's consider several instances of spiritual experiences, some with a physiological component, in the context of communion. Author and ministry leader John Sandford told me two that happened to him. As a pastor in a denomination that was starting to endorse anti-Biblical positions, he had a heavy heart while attending a regional denominational conference in Seattle.[94]

> I went to St. Patrick's Cathedral for morning mass. At this point [the late 1950s] they were still serving the wafer only. Both mornings, as I swallowed it, it was like coffee that was too hot, I could track it all the way down my throat to my stomach. When it reached my stomach, it exploded in glory that touched every cell in my body! It happened two days in a row—that gave me the strength to go through the days, listening to junk.
>
> Another time, I had to travel cross-country to teach. I had a long layover at the Chicago O'Hare Airport. A friend took me to… noon mass. I was suffering a kidney attack. I was having great pains in my back, affecting my

---

94   Personal conversation with John Sandford, April 4, 2015.

whole body. Again, I was served only the wafer—when
I took it, all pain left my body, and I was totally healed!

He also related another occasion, when he was in Sydney, Australia,
attending an ecumenical gathering.

I'd been invited by Servants of Jesus, a fellowship who
are eighty percent Roman Catholic and twenty percent
Protestant. I attended mass, and received both the bread
and the cup. Nothing seemed to happen in the moment I
received the elements, but as I turned to walk back to my
seat, they burst inside me and I was irradiated with the
Lord's presence—particularly with love. A friend said: "I
saw it hit you today, didn't it!"

Sandford told about a friend who was getting ready for her daugh-
ter's wedding:

Meanwhile, many miles away in Canada, another daugh-
ter's husband was in the hospital, in very serious condition. She left the wedding preparations, drove five hours to
the hospital, and looked for a priest (I don't know whether
Roman Catholic or Episcopalian). She asked him, "Do you
believe it's the real presence of the Lord in the sacrament?"

"Yes, it's the real presence." Together they went to
her son-in-law's hospital room. He was almost comatose.
He couldn't receive the wafer, he couldn't drink from the
cup; so the priest took a swab and painted his lips with
the wine! Glory descended, and the man came out of the
coma and was healed without any need of an operation!

Mother Teresa's life is referred to often as an example of following our Lord. Much of her encouragement in the Lord occurred in the context of the Lord's Supper. For instance, she related to her archbishop, when she was writing to ask permission to start a new order of nuns:

> One day at Holy Com. [Communion] I heard the same voice very distinctly—*"I want Indian nuns, victims of My love, who would be Mary and Martha, who would be so very united to Me as to radiate My love on souls. I want free nuns covered with My poverty of the Cross.—I want obedient nuns covered with My obedience of the Cross. I want full of love nuns covered with the Charity of the Cross. Wilt thou refuse to do this for Me?"*[95]

One wonders what experiences haven't been recorded because there's no particular framework for doing so. Steve Carpenter reported on a more widespread blessing that occurred as he focused on the Lord's Supper:

The result of that season of elevating in our hearts the place of the Lord's Table was that we began to take the Lord's Table all around the city of Fort Worth on a daily basis. (We did it every Sunday—we've done it every Sunday with every church I've ever pastored from the very beginning, coming right out of seminary. I believe it is that important.) But we began to take it every day. And there were homes, houses, all over the city, where you could take the Lord's Supper, and I want to tell you what began to break out from that—I hadn't intended this, I hadn't even thought about it—but we began to have a visitation of healing grace into our midst. We began to see incurable, terminal, illnesses healed. We

95   *Mother Teresa: Come Be My Light—The Private Writings of the "Saint of Calcutta,"* ed. Brian Kolodiejchuk (New York: Wheeler Publishing, 2007), 91.

saw a malignant brain tumor healed—instantly. We
began to see a visitation of the grace of God that over-
whelmed us. And I had not originally made that connection. I had not done this to try and get God to come
as a healing God. That was a by-product of simply seeking His presence. . . . The result of that for me was that I
began to see that there is much more that goes on in this
institution which Jesus has left with His church. If we
will give ourselves to this we will see breakthrough in
the Spirit that we have not discovered.[96]

The original Passover evidently had healing power. We see this same
dynamic from the other direction in Paul's comments about the Lord's
Supper in Corinth. When people are excluded from communion, he says,
"That is why many of you are weak and ill."[97] The Healing Rooms at
the International House of Prayer in Kansas City gave communion to
those seeking prayer for a season.[98] Tony Sanchez, who was active in the
healing ministry there, had met a woman from India through business
associates. She had a serious bowel condition and was planning to fly to
India with her husband to pursue healing. Tony suggested—why not fly
to Kansas City and get prayed for?

And so they said, "Okay"—total unbelievers, practicing
Hindus! So they come to the Healing Rooms. Tony meets
them and takes them in and begins to take them through
an explanation of the Table of the Lord. . . . "Let me explain
to you what it's about: The blood is about—God wants to

---

96   Steve Carpenter. "The Lord's Supper," audio CD (Kansas City, Missouri: Friends
      of the Bridegroom, Oct. 2003) #1.
97   1 Corinthians 11:30a, ESV.
98   Kevin Matthews, "The Lord's Table," audio CD (Kansas City, Missouri, Interna-
      tional House of Prayer, circa 2006).

forgive you for all your sins, and the body is about that God wants to heal you physically, because these are the two benefits of why Jesus died. And I want you to know God wants you to take this." Now some people say, 'Oooooh, you can't give communion to an unbeliever!?' Go and read some of Luther and Calvin's writings; they fought for it. . . . So he's [Tony is] leading them through as we've taught them to do, and then he says this to them. . . . "Listen, we would like for you to receive this, but I want you to understand this, if you receive this bread and if you receive this cup, and you eat and drink it, what you're doing is you're not receiving bread and wine—you're receiving Jesus. Would you like to do that?"[99] . . . and they say, "Okay" and so he ministers the communion to them and they get saved, both of them get saved, and then he prays for them for healing and they come back to the healing meeting Thursday night and she gets completely healed. Now, they're back in Phoenix, in a church, practicing Christians, loving the Lord and she's completely healed because someone just allowed the table to preach and said "Listen, this is for you."

"Expectancy" is an attitude of heart—excited, hopeful, and full of trust, without specific conditions. "Expectation" is when someone is looking for a particular result, a specific action or condition. May the attitude of our hearts be one of expectancy without expectations! That allows our Lord to bless us in the way He wants to—including in the sharing of His Supper.

---

99 Kevin Matthews made an aside here as part of telling the story: "See how simple that is? . . . It's this easy: This is His body. This is His blood. The table preaches all of its own. But we hid it away in a corner, and said to unbelievers, 'This isn't for you. This is the club meal. You gotta be part of the club!' It ought to be at the very doorway of the church, saying "This is for you— forgiveness and healing!"

How come there aren't more reports of obvious fruit resulting from Lord's Supper services? It may be tied to our lack of expectancy. And sometimes the fruit is hard to describe but nonetheless real in terms of human connections and relationships that continue to express love for our Lord over the long haul. Here's an instance from church history— a communion service was a key moment in the birth of the Moravian movement. The Moravians were a remarkable movement in pioneering missions to other people groups and a holistic view of following Jesus.

A young nobleman, Count Zinzendorf, had a large estate in southern Germany near Dresden, and he'd allowed refugees from religious disputes to settle there. In 1727, these refugees were disputing among themselves, as well as with the nearby Lutherans, who had for a century-and-a-half been "the Establishment church" in that area.

One refugee said the pastor of the local Lutheran church was "The False Prophet," and his host, Count Zinzendorf, was "The Beast" in the book of Revelation! That gives us an idea of the tone of the disputes![100] Through prayer, confrontation, and leadership by Count Zinzendorf, the Christians in that area learned, step by step, to love each other in true sincerity. Pastor Rothe of the local Lutheran church invited them all to set the seal upon this growth in unity by joining in the celebration of Holy Communion at Berthelsdorf Church on Monday, August 13. Here's the account:

> All who had quarreled in the days gone by made a covenant of loyalty and love. They entered the building, the service began... and then at one and the same moment, all present, rapt in deep devotion, were stirred by the mystic wondrous touch of a power which none could define or understand. There in Berthelsdorf Parish Church, they attained at last the firm conviction that they were one in Christ; and there,

---

100   E. H. Broadbent, *The Pilgrim Church*, (Basingstoke, United Kingdom: Pickering & Inglis. Originally published 1931, 1985 edition), 274–276.

above all, they believed and felt that on them, . . . had rested
the purifying fire of the Holy Ghost. . . .

> They walked with God in peace and love,
> But failed with one another;
> While sternly for the faith they strove,
> Brother fell out with brother;
> But He in Whom they put their trust,
> Who knew their frames, that they were dust,
> Pitied and healed their weakness.
> He found them in His house of prayer,
> With one accord assembled,
> And so revealed His presence there,
> They wept for joy and trembled;
> One cup they drank, one bread they brake,
> One baptism shared, one language spake,
> Forgiving and forgiven.
> Then they went forth with tongues of flame,
> In one blest theme delighting,
> The love of Jesus and His name,
> God's children all uniting!
> That love, our theme and watchword still;
> That law of love may we fulfil,
> And love as we are loved.

The next step was to see that the blessing was not
lost. For this purpose the Brethren, a few days later,
arranged a system of Hourly Intercession . . . . The whole
day was carefully mapped out, and each Brother or Sis-
ter took his or her turn. This prayer union lasted without
interruption for over a hundred and twenty years.[101]

---

101   J. E. Hutton, *History of the Moravian Church*, (London: Moravian Publication
Office, 1909), 209–211. The poem is by Moravian poet James Montgomery.

Another turning point in a group's experience was related by a missionary to Brazil during the 1960s–1980s:

> We had gathered around our dining room table for another one of Carol's soup suppers. Under normal circumstances we would have moved into the living room for our time in the Scriptures and prayer. But that evening, we did something we'd never done before.
>
> Carol and Sonia cleared the dishes off the table, leaving only our wineglasses and the bread plate. I reminded the group that Jesus had used these two things on the table in one of his final teaching sessions with his disciples. I then made the following suggestion: "Before we divide and share this bread and drink the last of the wine, I would like us to reflect for a moment and then share how our lives have been affected by what Jesus did for us on the cross." I could never have imagined what followed, nor will I ever forget it. One by one those young Brazilians, now devoted followers of Jesus Christ, shared from the depths of their hearts. Quietly, with voices choked with emotion, some with tears streaming down their faces, they offered their praise and thanksgiving for what God had done in their lives, for the love and acceptance they were experiencing in their marriages and from the group. We spent the rest of the evening around that table, in a powerful time of worship and adoration.[102]

Sometimes the effect of the Lord's Supper on someone is observable

---

102   Ken Lottis and Jim Petersen, *Will This Rock in Rio? Finding God in an Urban Culture* (Colorado Springs, Colorado: NavPress. 2010), 159–160.

to others. Psychologist and author Robert Coles relates this about French intellectual Simone Weil:

> Right after the Passion of Christ entered her being, she noticed a young man. "There was a young English Catholic there from whom I gained my first idea of the supernatural power of the sacraments because of the truly angelic radiance with which he seemed to be clothed after going to communion."[103]

Others' experiences of the Lord Supper feature receiving a greater revelation of Jesus. Here is an example of a dramatic spiritual revelation coming during the Lord's Supper, related by author Ana Mendez Ferrell:

> Once, while eating of His flesh, I saw Him nailed to the cross with His open wounds and disfigured face. I could see each one of my sins in each one of His wounds with my name written on them. Then, I heard His voice clearly say to me, "This is My body which was broken because of you." A horrible shudder ran through my being when I realized that my sins crucified the Son of God. I, Ana, with my deeds brutalized my beloved Jesus. I put Him to death. We killed Him. . . . The primitive church lived this every day. As they broke bread among the brethren, they remembered what their sins had done to the body of the Lord. They gazed into each others' eyes as they saw how they had wounded Jesus' body. Their souls lived it every day. They felt it in their hearts, and it transformed them.[104]

103   Robert Coles, *Simone Weil—A Modern Pilgrimage* (Reading, Massachusetts: Addison-Wesley Publishing. 1987), 118.
104   Ana Mendez Ferrell. *Eat My Flesh, Drink My Blood*, 1st English ed. (Pontre Vedra, Florida: E & A International, 2006), 101–102.

Another experience Ferrell related this way:

> I had just taken Communion, and I was enjoying deep meditation on my Lord, when my spirit was carried to the Holy of Holies in Heaven. The Ark of the Covenant glowed. It was full of a shining energy that is difficult to describe. It was like an incredibly dense, churning fire. Rays of light beamed out of it. Then I saw Jesus enter in. I could only see His white, glistening clothing. His face was hidden behind the shining glory that surrounded Him. A formless mass, like a wafting, floating liquid was in front of Him, moving towards the Ark. It was His Blood. Suddenly, He puts it upon the mercy seat, between the two cherubim that guard the cover. A magnificent power was produced in that instant. It was like seeing the explosion of an atomic bomb. Everything shook fiercely in heaven and earth. An endless thunder filled the entire place. . . . . I felt as if thousands of volts of electricity were going through me. My entire body turned red. His blood was in every atom of my being . . . . I saw it circulate as if there were hundreds of lightning bolts running through my body. I thought I was literally going to die. It was much too powerful for a mortal, ordinary being like me. His voice resounded strongly, saying, "My Father has received My Blood and now, it has united with His spirit. Receive the life in My blood.". . . I came back from that experience and . . . I would never again think of the blood of Jesus as a ritual, or a verbal proclamation.[105]

---

105   Ibid., 48–50.

CHAPTER 9

STUCK ON REMEMBERING ME–
NOT OUR LORD

I THOUGHT I had to make myself worthy to receive the Lord's Supper—not simply receive it in a worthy manner.

> Whoever, therefore, eats the bread or drinks the cup of the Lord in an unworthy manner will be guilty concerning the body and blood of the Lord. Let a person examine himself, then, and so eat of the bread and drink of the cup. For anyone who eats and drinks without discerning the body eats and drinks judgment on himself.[106]

Memory can be a harsh master. True—it can also liberate. If we approach the Lord's Supper and are reminded of the reality of God all around us, remembering can liberate. But when we remember only ourselves, we can take on a terrible yoke.

As I'm writing this, I'm in the process of helping my mother move out of our family home of fifty years. Mementos from my youth bring up lots of memories. Some of those memories bring up "What if" questions: "What if I had gone that way instead of this way?" "What if I'd done *this*?" Unrealized potential is a great burden. As I remember different

---

106   1 Corinthians 11:27–29, ESV.

unrealized potentialities I end up being dragged down by the sheer weight of so many possibilities.

In the same way, many times I've given the enemy chains to bind me when I've approached the Lord's Supper. I've taken the instruction to "examine" myself and gotten stuck on the examination table! I'm remembering sin, or even just temptations. I've never gotten past that self-examination to focus on the Lord. However, as Mike Mason puts it, "The communion service should emphasize our union with Christ, not our disunion."[107] Agreed!

What does "examine ourselves" really mean?

The word translated "examine" is *dokimazos*.[108] Just nine verses earlier, Paul used the noun form of the word *dokimo*, as he introduced his thoughts on how the Corinthians were conducting the Lord's Supper. How is it translated there?

> In the following directives I have no praise for you, for your meetings do more harm than good. In the first place, I hear that when you come together as a church, there are divisions among you, and to some extent I believe it. No doubt there have to be differences among you to show which of you have God's *approval*.[109]

So *dokimo*, the noun form, equals approval! The verb form, *dokimazos*, is used two other times in 1 Corinthians:

---

107   Mike Mason, *Champagne for the Soul*, (Colorado Springs: Waterbrook Press, 2003), 86.

108   *Strong's Concordance* gives this definition: "to test (literally or figuratively); by implication to approve: allow, discern, examine, x [a Greek idiom] like, (ap-) prove, try."

109   1 Corinthians 11:17–19, NIV. The ESV concludes this sentence this way: "there must be factions among you in order that those who are genuine among you may be recognized." The NABre says: "there have to be factions among you in order that [also] those who are approved among you may become known."

If any man builds on this foundation using gold, silver, costly stones, wood, hay or straw, their work will be shown for what it is, because the Day will bring it to light. It will be revealed with fire, and the fire will *test* the quality of each person's work.[110]

And when I arrive, I shall send those whom you have approved with letters of recommendation to take your gracious gift to Jerusalem.[111]

Here's one of the three times *dokimazos* is used in 2 Corinthians, "In addition, we are sending with them our brother who has often *proved* to us in many ways that he is zealous, and now even more so because of his great confidence in you."[112] It's interesting to note that Paul uses a completely different Greek word as he concludes 2 Corinthians: "Examine yourselves, to see whether you are in the faith."[113] Has the close proximity of the two passages and the use of the same English word in many translations confused these entirely separate directions?

Now that we see the range of meaning the word *dokimazos* has (examine—prove—test—approve), how does this apply to a person in the Lord's Supper? Could a believer flunk the test and not be approved?

First, should the proving process Paul asks for be administered by someone else? No, Paul says, "let a person examine himself."[114]

When Paul asked believers to do that, did he ever expect people to conclude they weren't "worthy" of the Lord's Supper? He doesn't say participants need to "feel" like they're worthy. It's certainly not a matter of our emotional condition prior to receiving the elements.

---

110   1 Corinthians 3:12–13, NIV.
111   1 Corinthians 16:3, NABre. NIV uses "approve"; ESV says "those whom you accredit."
112   2 Corinthians 8:22, NIV. ESV says "our brother whom we have often tested"; NABre: "whom we often tested in many ways."
113   2 Corinthians 13:5a, ESV. The Greek word here is *peirazo*.
114   1 Corinthians 11:28, ESV.

He doesn't make any mention of confession, although no doubt that's part of walking in friendship with our Lord Jesus. Certainly I'd advise people who are approaching the Lord's Supper who think they're unworthy of it to consider their state for a moment, ask the Lord to forgive them for any specifics that come to mind, and then—carry on and enter in![115]

It's vital that we look at Paul's bottom line to understand his language asking us to prove/examine ourselves. After describing the problem of "not discerning" the Lord's body *and* receiving it in a worthy manner, Paul gives his conclusion. It's a narrow set of directions. It's to ask for the most basic courtesy, "Therefore, my brothers, when you come together to eat, *wait for one another.* If anyone is hungry, he should eat at home, so that your meetings may not result in judgment."[116]

If you apply these directions to most church gatherings, it's almost impossible to see the problem he was addressing. What brought forth his injunction to examine/test/prove ourselves?

Paul was addressing a situation where there was an actual honest-to-goodness meal—a covered-dish supper, in effect. But the rich (who could set their own hours, and thus come early) were eating everything, and by the time those in need (particularly the servants and slaves) arrived

---

115 Author John Sandford says that holding unforgiveness should keep someone from taking part. Our Lord made clear the eternal consequences of unforgiveness through the story of the unforgiving servant. It concludes: "Then his master summoned him and said to him, 'You wicked servant! I forgave you all that debt because you pleaded with me. And should not you have had mercy on your fellow servant, as I had mercy on you?' And in anger his master delivered him to the jailers, until he should pay all his debt. So also my heavenly Father will do to every one of you, if you do not forgive your brother from your heart" (Matthew 18:32–36, ESV). Any opportunity to reflect on our spiritual condition, including the Lord's Supper, is a great time to see if we hold bitterness against someone or something. But I don't see Paul's directions indicating this focus. His words spring from his anger that there's division (lack of concern for one another) in eating the Lord's Supper and conclude with the remedy that we should wait for one another to eat. His words don't focus on other sins.

116 1 Corinthians 11:33–34, NABre; emphasis added.

at the meeting, there was nothing left to eat. Paul's passion was that the needy be treated with dignity.

Instead, his directions have sometimes resulted in people avoiding the very celebration that would bring the life they need. Here's an example that applies to anyone who gets stuck on the examination table like I used to:

> This story has been told of the famous Scottish theologian John Duncan, of New College in Edinburgh. At communion one Sunday, when the elements came to a sixteen-year-old girl, she suddenly turned her head aside. She motioned for the elder to take the cup away, that she couldn't drink it. John Duncan reached his long arm over, touched her shoulder and said tenderly, "Take it lassie, it's for sinners!"[117]

The examination, or approval, process Paul is calling for can be likened to airport security screening. Even if you bring a chainsaw as carry-on luggage, as a few misguided people have done, officials will confiscate the chainsaw but you will still pass the test and make it on to your flight. It's just a matter of leaving something behind—there's never any question what's important: It's the flight!

"But let a man prove himself, and so let him eat of the bread and drink of the cup."[118]

In other words, it's that simple: Confirm your standing with our Lord and partake.

---

117 Michael Green, ed., *Illustrations for Biblical Preaching* (Grand Rapids: Baker Book House, 1989), 75.

118 1 Corinthians 11:28, Revised Version, 1881. This revision of the Authorized, or King James, version was done by British and American scholars at the invitation of the Church of England. It was the first official update in 270 years. One comment sees the translation as "excessively literal"—which is fascinating in regard to this verse in particular!

EXAMINATION AND APPROVAL

The Lord's Supper on Colonial Pennsylvania's frontier

The great event of the church year was the communion season, which was generally observed twice a year, sometimes only once. The Thursday before communion was a fast day or at least a day of prayer. On Saturday a preparatory sermon was preached to "fix the truths," and the members in good standing were given "tokens," which were discs of lead with the initials of the congregation stamped on them. Three or four ministers took part in the services. First came the "action sermon" by the regular pastor. The next sermon was devoted to "fencing the tables," barring from communion all who were guilty of any of a great number of sins. Then came "the welcome to communion" which let down the bars and admitted into grace those who had been shut out. A final service Monday morning completed the celebration.[119]

This approach combines intense spiritual preparation with the truth that our Lord wants all of us to participate in obeying His command: "Do this in remembrance of me." How can we duplicate this approach in our current church culture?

---

119 Samuel Culbertson Orr, *Ancestors Antecedents Recollections of Samuel Culbertson Orr,* (Buhl, Idaho: published by the author, 1964), 39. Church of Scotland minister and former theology professor William Storrar explained to me in a personal conversation March 13, 2018, that elders reviewing who should receive tokens examined both a person's understanding of the faith and their behavior.

CHAPTER 10

SHOULD OBEDIENCE
BE RESTRICTED?

Who can lead the Lord's Supper?
Should we restrict participation?

DO WE NEED an ordained pastor to celebrate the Lord's Supper?

The first time I ever even thought about this question I'd just met a young Roman Catholic lady and found out she wanted the priesthood to be open to females. I asked her why.

Her answer astounded me, since at this point I didn't place any importance on the act. She simply answered, with deep feeling: "So I can celebrate the sacrament!"[120]

I couldn't miss her intensity. I started turning this over in my mind. Who does the Bible say can lead a Lord's Supper? Was there anything preventing me from leading the sacrament? My thinking had certainly been limited by my experience.

As far as I've been able to find in the Bible, the only thing limiting my leading the Lord's Supper is my own spiritual inertia (a polite word for laziness!). Yet many who call on the name of Jesus would differ and say someone needs to be ordained, to be officially authorized to represent Jesus Christ, in declaring the bread to be His body. There's no clear statement limiting certain functions (like leading communion or forgiving

---

120   See the sidebar for a discussion of the term "sacrament."

sins in terms of John 20:22–23[121]) to ordained clergy.[122] The basis for restricting communion leadership to those who are ordained depends upon allowing a church authority to set such limits. The question I would raise is: What's been the fruit of such limits? Do they encourage the New Testament atmosphere of expressing spontaneous devotion to our Lord, joy and relational connection with one another?

There does remain a role for church leadership—Paul took a role in establishing order in the Lord's Supper. Church leaders are to guard the flock. Speaking as such a leader, we're also to encourage and equip all believers to teach others to obey all that Jesus commanded. In fact, that's the best way to guard a flock, to be on the "offensive" rather than the "defensive." We're certainly not to limit anyone's obedience to the Lord's commands—including His command to celebrate the supper in remembrance of Him! Of course, as my lead pastor Geoffrey Winkler has taught me, we're to teach obedience as sons and daughters—out of responsive love, rather than as employees and servants! The moment we consider celebrating the Lord's Supper in smaller settings, we realize how appropriate it is for heads of households to lead the meal, or even to ask someone else to lead it—without any need for ordination or licensing![123]

But I've made mistakes in "guarding the flock." One was actually a two-part mistake. Not only did I want to restrict the Lord's Supper to people I knew were believers, I wanted to restrict the Supper to believers who were living lives above reproach.

Shouldn't we restrict participation? What do we do about guests who

---

121   "And when He had said this, He breathed on them and said to them, 'Receive the holy Spirit. Whose sins you forgive are forgiven them, and whose sins you retain are retained'" (John 20:22–23, NABre).

122   I recognize some read passages conferring authority to the original eleven disciples—like the authority to forgive sins, as establishing a hierarchy whose approval was needed to pass on that authority—but that seems a strained reading of those texts.

123   Household heads as the leaders of communion celebrations is consistent with the pattern God established for Passover.

aren't part of the Body of Christ? An extreme version of the problem occurred in the early church, and it's described in Jude's letter:

> For certain people have crept in unnoticed who long ago were designated for this condemnation, ungodly people, who pervert the grace of our God into sensuality and deny our only Master and Lord, Jesus Christ. . . . These are hidden reefs at your love feasts, as they feast with you without fear, shepherds feeding themselves.[124]

Jude is warning his readers that their love feasts, which no doubt included the Lord's Supper, have been infiltrated by rebels against Christ. When the Lord's Supper is served in large groups, it's quite possible someone will be served who isn't part of the body of Christ. Unbelievers can't participate in the spiritual reality of the event. If they eat the bread or share the cup, they can't be part of the spiritual transaction because they aren't in the "one loaf" that Paul speaks of in 1 Corinthians 10. Part of the problem is that their presence won't be visible—they'll be "unnoticed."

Jude wrote his letter specifically to ask his readers "to defend the faith that God has entrusted once for all time to his holy people. I say this because some ungodly people have wormed their way into your churches."[125] But how does Jude ask his readers to defend the faith? He doesn't suggest trying to exclude them from the love feasts. He gives us much more general direction that applies all the time—when we serve the Lord's Supper and when we don't. After encouraging believers to build up their own faith and awareness of God's love, the only directions in Jude's letter that could possibly apply to the "hidden reefs at your love feasts" are these instructions: "And have mercy on those who doubt; save

---

124   Jude 1:4, 12a, ESV.
125   Jude 3b–4a, NLT.

others by snatching them out of the fire; to others show mercy with fear, hating even the garment stained by the flesh."[126]

I can appreciate what a wonderful opportunity the Lord's Supper appears to provide for leaders to set standards and require certain behavior. I've done it. My wife and I were leading an "on fire" home group. We had started out meeting with one other couple. In a few months we needed to move our meetings to their backyard, because the forty people who were now coming couldn't fit in their home! I was convinced that one of our attenders was a false brother—I knew from his friend that he lived a sinful lifestyle, though he was portraying himself as a committed believer. So, rather than asking him privately about his lifestyle,[127] I used the Lord's Supper as the occasion to address it. I preached before we had the bread and the cup on how we needed to confess our sins (to the point, one friend said later, that I seemed to be forcing a confession out of everyone!)[128] The "false brother" never returned to our group. Was my exhortation on confession of sin a proper use of the Lord's Supper and a victory for protecting our body? Or was it fear of individual confrontation on my part that ended up driving away someone who needed help?

On reflection, shouldn't a leader's approach be like that of Philip?

---

126 Jude 22–23, ESV.
127 "If your brother sins against you, go and tell him his fault, between you and him alone. If he listens to you, you have gained your brother. But if he does not listen, take one or two others along with you, that every charge may be established by the evidence of two or three witnesses. If he refuses to listen to them, tell it to the church. And if he refuses to listen even to the church, let him be to you as a Gentile and a tax collector" (Matthew 18:15–17, ESV). While the "false brother" didn't sin directly against me, the principle this passage teaches of private confrontation was a better approach. A few judicious questions would have been a great place to start. "The purpose in a man's heart is like deep water, but a man of understanding will draw it out." (Proverbs 20:5, ESV). "The one who states his case first seems right, until the other comes and examines him" (Proverbs 18:17, ESV).
128 If I'd been quick thinking, I could have responded that some church traditions do require confession before the Lord's Supper (e.g., the Roman Catholic).

When the Ethiopian eunuch asked Philip to baptize him, Philip didn't wait and require any added commitment or other members' approval. He didn't ask a series of questions to insure the eunuch understood this step of obedience. At most, Philip simply gave him one requirement: "If you believe with all your heart, you may."[129] (I say "at most," since those words aren't included in all the Greek manuscripts.) In a similar way, if people step forward to take part in the Lord's Supper, we don't need to interview them at length to determine their heart before granting them the bread and the cup.[130] The lead-up to sharing the bread and the cup can be a good time to make clear the separation which is hidden to our physical eyes—the separation between the saved and the lost. We can say something like this:

"As we approach the table of the Lord, we want to make clear this is open to anyone because Jesus' invitation to follow Him is open to anyone. At the same time, we wouldn't want you to be under a false impression that you're a believer because you obeyed Him in this one area. The word of God says that we can know for certain that we've passed from death to life—that we have eternal life. If you don't know that for sure, may I invite you to come talk with us following this service?"[131]

The Lord's Supper is a multisensory presentation of the good news that Jesus came in the flesh and died a violent, sacrificial death for us. We proclaim Christ when we do the Supper—both to believers and unbelievers. But as we saw earlier, the benefits of the Supper require faith, since one can only truly participate in the Body as part of the

---

129 Acts 8:37, NKJV. This verse isn't in the earliest Greek manuscripts which other English translations of the Bible use today.

130 See Appendix 1, "Why Offer Communion to Everyone at a Gathering?"

131 There are a number of assurances given in 1 John so people can know they have "passed from death to life." For instance, "But whoever keeps His word, truly the love of God is perfected in him. By this we know that we are in Him" (1 John 2:5, ESV). Or another, "We know that we have passed from death to life, because we love each other" (1 John 3:14, NIV).

Body![132] One can only share a testamental meal by being an heir of the testament!

Some may be concerned about an unbeliever coming under judgment because he or she takes part. I don't see that as a concern at all. Paul says "many of you" and "we" in the passage about judgment. His concern is that his *fellow believers* will be judged, "For anyone who eats and drinks without discerning the body eats and drinks judgment on himself. That is why *many of you* are weak and ill, and some have died. But if *we* judged ourselves truly, *we* would not be judged."[133]

It's fascinating the goal of this judgment would actually benefit unbelievers: "But when we are judged by the Lord, we are *disciplined so that we may not be condemned along with the world.*"[134] Paul is addressing believers. This is confirmed when he makes a contrast between "we" and "the world." It's believers who can come under this judgment. This is consistent with the book of Hebrews. It says the Father's discipline is really a paternity test—only believers are disciplined by the Lord.[135]

This description of God's practice of judging and disciplining us provides part of the answer to why the Lord allows suffering. We can apply this brief description to many situations. Illness and death can be seen as discipline the Lord allows, which protects us from being satisfied with

---

132   "The cup of blessing that we bless, is it not a participation in the blood of Christ? The bread that we break, is it not a participation in the body of Christ? Because there is one bread, we who are many are one body, for we all partake of the one bread" (1 Corinthians 10:16–17, ESV).

133   1 Corinthians 11:29–31, ESV; emphasis added.

134   1 Corinthians 11:32, ESV; emphasis added.

135   "'For the Lord disciplines the one he loves, and chastises every son whom he receives.' It is for discipline that you have to endure. God is treating you as sons. For what son is there whom his father does not discipline? If you are left without discipline, in which all have participated, then you are illegitimate children and not sons" (Hebrews 12:6–8, ESV). I recognize that our Lord judges nations and groups throughout the Old Testament, so I'm not saying unbelievers in our day can't suffer judgment—but this would be distinct from discipline, which is what Paul says occurs in the context of the Lord's Supper.

what the world has to offer. I'm more focused on eternity at a funeral or memorial service than on other occasions. Sickness can wake me up afresh to my frailty, my finitude—my need for God!

Let's return to the unbelievers' situation. They have a much more serious problem in receiving the Lord's Supper than discipline which keeps them from being condemned with the world. I'd hope all unbelievers would come under discipline that keeps them from being condemned! If this is what actually happens, then let's serve every unbeliever communion.

The unbelievers' problem is that they're part of "the world"! I would see the major concern not as possible discipline by their Heavenly Father, but that on occasion some might be deluded into remaining in unbelief precisely because they've taken part in the Lord's Supper and think they're safe. Jesus does describe some people at the final judgment who may be deluded—or at least want to make a case that they're believers because they did particular things:

> On that day many will say to me, "Lord, Lord, did we not prophesy in your name, and cast out demons in your name, and do many mighty works in your name? And then will I declare to them, 'I never knew you; depart from me, you workers of lawlessness."[136]

Those who lead the Lord's Supper face a dilemma, particularly in large meetings. We don't want any unbelievers to be deluded by their own participation—but we should be more concerned that all those who are in Christ receive the Supper. The actual problem Paul railed against in 1 Corinthians wasn't that some unbelievers were taking part—it was that some believers didn't get to take part! The failure to include the poor in the Lord's Supper led to the Lord disciplining members of the Corinthian church by allowing sickness.

---

136   Matthew 7:22–23, ESV.

Still we want to make clear that without faith in Christ, there's no point in taking part. Or is there? If we're proclaiming Christ by our action in sharing the bread and the cup—maybe there is! Could the opening story in this book happen?

No doubt because it's a corporate act, the Lord's Supper has been the focus of some occasions of church discipline. Leaders will refuse to serve someone as "excommunication" from a body. For instance, in the early days of the United States, some people in western Pennsylvania were upset at the whiskey tax, which led to the Whiskey Insurrection, a rebellion against the federal government. Governing authorities responded by asking for people to take an oath of allegiance. One pastor, the so-called "Presbyterian pope" in this heavily Presbyterian area, postponed communion until after the time of taking the oath of allegiance "as an intimation to his people that they had better sign up or else."[137]

What are we to make of focusing church discipline on excluding the offender from the Lord's Supper? Certainly Paul did tell us to not eat with false brothers:

> I wrote to you in my letter not to associate with sexually immoral people—not at all meaning the sexually immoral of this world, or the greedy and swindlers, or idolaters, since then you would need to go out of the world. But now I am writing to you not to associate with anyone who bears the name of brother if he is guilty of sexual immorality or greed, or is an idolater, reviler, drunkard, or swindler—not even to eat with such a one. For what have I to do with judging outsiders? Is it not those inside the church whom you are to judge? God judges those outside. "Purge the evil person from among you."[138]

137 Samuel Culbertson Orr, *Ancestors Antecedents Recollections of Samuel Culbertson Orr*, (Buhl, Idaho: published by author, 1964), 38.
138 1 Corinthians 5:9–13, ESV.

Paul's directions are so sweeping that I fear they are seldom referenced, much less carried out. They certainly don't point to focusing on an exclusion from the Lord's Supper as the fulfillment or sum total of church discipline. Arthur Cochrane does put the two together with the celebration of the Lord's Supper:

> From what has been learned about *diakonia* [Greek for "serving"], it is evident that the Lord's Supper, as an act of love, cannot be restricted to baptized members of the body of Christ. The Table of Lord may be fenced against "one who bears the name of brother if he is guilty of immorality" and idolatry; but it may not be fenced against immoral and idolatrous unbelievers (1 Cor. 5:9–13). Paul counted upon the attendance of unbelievers and outsiders at the gatherings of the church for thanksgiving (1 Cor. 14:16, 23–25). As Jesus received and ate with sinners, as the father received the prodigal son before any confession of sin was made, so the church will extend hospitality to sinners and strangers.[139]

Basic hospitality can guide us in offering communion to guests, trusting the Spirit of God will keep people from being deceived about their eternal destiny.

---

139 Arthur C. Cochrane, *Eating and Drinking with Jesus—An Ethical and Biblical Inquiry,* (Philadelphia: Westminster Press, 1974), 90–91. I only found his work toward the completion of my own writing. I mention this because some of this scholar's thinking is so similar to my own, I don't want to be accused of plagiarism!

SACRAMENT OR ORDINANCE?

Is communion a "sacrament" or an "ordinance?" Some see the Lord's Supper as necessary for salvation, and use the word "sacrament" to describe it. Others term it a "sacrament," but simply mean it's an action which imparts God's grace to people, or dedicates them to Himself, without being essential for one's salvation. The word "sacrament" doesn't occur in the Greek New Testament, but of course neither does "trinity."[140]

---

140 The definition of sacrament varies now and has varied over time. *Sacramentum* is used in the Latin Vulgate translation of the New Testament to translate the Greek word *mysterion* in Ephesians 5:32. In this passage, Paul says that what was talked about in the Old Testament, of a man and a woman becoming one flesh in marriage, is a *mysterion*. Joseph Grassi commented on this: "Mysterion is the Pauline word for 'God's long-hidden secret'. . . As understood here, it means that the verse in Genesis has a hidden meaning, only now understood. 'I mean in reference to Christ and the Church': The text of Genesis, which expresses the sacred nature of marriage, fore-shadowed in the bond of husband and wife the union of Christ and his spouse, the Church." Joseph A. Grassi, "The Letter to the Ephesians," from *The Jerome Biblical Commentary: The New Testament and Topical Articles,* Vol. II (Englewood Cliffs, NJ: Prentice-Hall, 1968), 349. Communion is certainly an act with hidden meaning which reveals something, but given the variety of meanings attached to *sacrament* now, another label seems preferable.

Others would see communion as a representation and reminder *ordained* by the Lord, thus "ordinance." These two words are labels for different beliefs about the Lord's Supper, reinforcing division between groups. Could we start using a third term, a Biblical term, as a step to allow differences in understanding of a mystery?

"Memorial" appeals to me. The words "Do this in remembrance of me," can just as well be translated "Do this as a memorial to me." While dead leaders have concrete or bronze memorials, a living God should have a living memorial. To me, this memorial is the fulfillment of this prophetic promise: "To the eunuchs who keep my Sabbaths, who choose what pleases me and hold fast to my covenant—to them I will give within my temple [where they couldn't go under the Law] and its walls a memorial and a name better than sons and daughters."[141]

---

141 Isaiah 56:4b–5b, NIV.

"WHAT IF?"

Another Dream of What Might Become

I t all started when Dewey, the Baptist pastor, got to thinking as he was studying church history: "If the Roman Catholics will offer me communion if I'm Orthodox, maybe I could get baptized as an Orthodox and bridge the gap myself—between the different traditions!"

So he went and met with Father Gregory. They had a delightful time getting to know each other, comparing notes on their spiritual journeys. But Dewey didn't get as far as asking to be baptized because Father Gregory said, "I can't offer you communion—I'm not in communion with you!" Particularly after the friendly start, his words were a shock to Dewey. The experience unnerved him from even thinking about the topic for some months. He went back to the drawing board. He pondered, why isn't anyone else bothered by the contradiction that believers are told we're one body? It's a clear statement in the Bible. Yet in the action that's supposed to demonstrate our unity, our being from one loaf, we don't demonstrate it?

Then one day, as Dewey was having coffee with Julius, the AME (African Methodist Episcopal) pastor in the city, he brought up the topic. After all, they could receive communion at each other's services—right? In a flash, Julius remembered something from his family's stories and a smile crossed his face: "What if we applied civil disobedience to mending the divide between believers?"

"What do you mean?" said Dewey.

"Ultimately, to the extent that the civil rights movement

worked, it worked because it appealed to people's consciences—that part of our hearts which is attuned to the Lord. We knew that no matter how prejudiced or bigoted a person appeared to be, or had been raised to be, or shaped to be, there was something in them—put there by God Almighty—that would respond to a higher call, an appeal to God's character."

Dewey was still puzzled, "Yeah . . . ?"

"So what if we applied that—at the grassroots level—to communion?"

So that's how it started. Julius called up Father Chase, of the nearby parish, and told him he and Dewey were planning to be at the 6 p.m. Roman Catholic mass Saturday. And Julius assured Father Chase, "Both Dewey and I believe in the real presence of the Lord Jesus in the action of communion."

That first time there was no fanfare, not even any spectators or friends along—just the two of them. Dewey's wife could tell it meant a lot to him, but Julius' wife just hoped he wouldn't be out too late. Father Chase, on the other hand, had had a rough week. His mind had been in turmoil ever since he'd taken that call from Julius. He'd known Julius from a couple of community meetings they'd both been at, and didn't think of him as antagonistic—but this, why this was like . . . !

But Father Chase was clear on what he had to do: Politely and firmly, as they came forward, he inserted himself in front of the server and gave each of them a blessing—but no wafer or cup. He was satisfied that night, and even took the time to write a note to his superior. But the next week—there they were again. And after the third week, he discovered he was tossing and turning as he went to sleep Saturday night!

That Tuesday he got a voicemail—someone he'd never heard of: "This is Pastor Paul over at Spring Meadows. I thought it only right to let you know that I'm planning to be at your service this Saturday and that I'd like to receive the bread and the cup. You see—I believe Jesus meant what He said when He said, 'This is my body.' So I hope you can include me."

"Why me?" Father Chase said to himself—and poured out his heart in prayer. Then he remembered praying several times for the uniting of the body of Christ. Did he, or was he imagining, the Lord saying: "I remember your prayer—I want to answer your prayer."

Of course, that Saturday Father Chase figured out who Pastor Paul was, because there was another fellow with Julius and Dewey. Dewey had evidently told Paul what he and Julius were doing. "Oh no," Father Chase had groaned inside—what if they each tell someone this next week? Or what happens if one of them doesn't look to be part of that group; and just appears to be a visitor from another parish? That could happen, too. Father Chase's fears appeared to be exaggerated as the next weekend it was only Paul. Julius and Dewey weren't there. Father Chase rested easy that night—the worst was over, he concluded. Their energy was dissipated and this question would go away.

Little did he know that Julius and Dewey had decided to go through the same exercise over at the Orthodox church! Their experience there was a little messier, as Father Gregory actually told them both, in front of those attending: "We're not in communion with you!"

The next week got even more awkward for Father Chase, because evidently Pastor Paul had shared what he was doing with the youth group at his church, and several of the youth showed up. One of them had the audacity to say in front of everyone there: "I believe Jesus is in the bread and the cup—why can't I receive?"

At that point, Father Chase stumbled. Looking back, he realized he should have kept his cool and repeated the same blessing he'd been giving each week. But instead he answered him, "Because you haven't been through our Rite of Christian Initiation of Adults class." The words just hung out there in space. They came back to haunt him the next week. Somehow, seemingly from nowhere the question formed in his mind: "Was heaven going to be that small?"

And little did he know that the stress could get worse. One of the attendants asked him that week, "How come we don't at least offer them to go through confirmation class?" Because—because—and Father Chase realized he was in a pickle. What if he did go to Dewey and Julius and give them the alternative of going through the class—and then what if they did? What if this got publicized? What if . . . ?[142]

---

142 Roman Catholic Canon Law 844 § 1-5 provide instances where communion can be served to non-catholics. For instance, § 4: "If there is danger of death or if, in the judgment of the diocesan Bishop of the Episcopal Conference, there is some other grave or pressing need, catholic ministers may lawfully administer these same sacraments to other Christians not in full communion with the catholic Church, who cannot approach a minister of their own community and who spontaneously ask for them, provided that they demonstrate the catholic faith in respect of these sacraments and are properly disposed." As one commentator noted, this is for "one time exceptional situations," not for regular connection between different members of the larger body of Christ.

WAS JUDAS THERE? OR JOHN MARK?

Luke's account has Jesus giving thanks—evidently at the beginning of the Passover meal and then breaking the bread and announcing, "This is my body, which is given for you. Do this in remembrance of me."[143] Later, perhaps immediately thereafter, Jesus gave Judas a piece of bread after John asked his master who would betray him.[144] It would have been odd for Jesus to break

---

143 Luke 22:19b, ESV.

144 "After saying these things, Jesus was troubled in his spirit, and testified, 'Truly, truly, I say to you, one of you will betray me.' The disciples looked at one another, uncertain of whom he spoke. One of his disciples, whom Jesus loved, was reclining at table at Jesus' side, so Simon Peter motioned to him to ask Jesus of whom he was speaking. So that disciple, leaning back against Jesus, said to him, 'Lord, who is it?' Jesus answered, 'It is he to whom I will give this morsel of bread when I have dipped it.' So when he had dipped the morsel, he gave it to Judas, the son of Simon Iscariot. Then after he had taken the morsel, Satan entered into him" (John 13:21–27a, ESV). Author John Sandford sees an expression of the salt covenant in Jesus giving Judas the piece of bread. Eating salt together (and bread would have contained salt) committed two parties to a reciprocal bond of friendship and protection. "Abijah stood on Mount Zemaraim, in the hill country of Ephraim, and said, "Jeroboam and all Israel, listen to me! Don't you know that the Lord, the God of Israel, has given the kingship of Israel to David and his descendants forever by a covenant of salt?'" (2 Chronicles 13:4–5, NIV). "Whatever is set aside from the holy offerings the Israelites present to the Lord I give to you and your sons and daughters as your perpetual share. It is an everlasting covenant of salt before the Lord for both you and your offspring" (Numbers 18:19, NIV). Sandford sees Jesus as saying: "'Judas, I know you are going to betray Me to My death this night, but on a covenant of

SHOULD OBEDIENCE BE RESTRICTED?   109

off a piece of bread before the blessing. It's possible—and this would have wonderful poetic significance—Judas didn't receive the new testamental cup as this came "after they had eaten."[145]

Was John Mark there? There's a passage describing Jesus' arrest in the garden of Gethsemane where John Mark, the author of the Gospel of Mark, says, "And a young man followed him, with nothing but a linen cloth about his body. And they [the guards who'd arrested Jesus] seized him, but he left the linen cloth and ran away naked."[146]

This detail isn't included in the other gospels. This supports the conclusion of many commentators that John Mark was talking about himself. One likely explanation of his being at Gethsemane is that Judas had first led the group arresting Jesus to the upper room, where he'd left Jesus. If the meal was at John Mark's home, he would have been awakened by the commotion, realized the danger Jesus was in, and rushed to Gethsemane in just the linen covering he'd been sleeping with to warn Jesus that the arrest mob was coming. No doubt if the Last Supper was eaten at John Mark's home, he assisted with or at least looked in on the meal.

---

salt I promise to protect and preserve your soul from now on!'....His betrayer, by eating with Jesus, was entering into the salt covenant to be...true to Him, but he was breaking that sacred covenant even as he made it." *Loving Jesus More.* (Battle Ground, Washington: BT Johnson Publishing. 2017) p. 21, 195.

145 Luke 22:20a. The next verse implies Judas was still at the table, but Jesus may have said this earlier than the cup taken after the meal, as John's account says Judas left after being given a piece of bread, apparently while the meal was still going on (John 13:21-30).

146 Mark 14:51-52, ESV.

CHAPTER 11

WHAT ABOUT THE CHILDREN?

DO WE ALLOW children to obey our Lord's direction?

Some advocate that children shouldn't be involved until they can understand. Why? We regularly hold up, as examples of faith, acts of obedience which preceded understanding: Noah building a boat when there had never been rain; Abram going to a place he hadn't been, offering his promised son Isaac as a sacrifice; Moses' mother putting her baby on a raft. . . . When it comes to the Lord's Supper, what do we as adults "understand"? If we admit that at the core of the Lord's Supper is a divine mystery, what are we requiring children to understand?

There's no dispute that early celebrations of the Lord's Supper included children, as described in Roman Catholic scholar Ed Foley's fictional account of such an occasion:

> To Jacob's surprise, his lone guest mesmerized the children. How quiet they became as Ruben unfolded stories of Jesus curing a boy with palsy, mending relationships between quarreling siblings, multiplying bread and fish for thousands, and sharing a final meal with his inner circle of friends. They sat transfixed as Ruben whispered the story of Jesus' trial, crucifixion, and burial. Then there were the events of the third day—most astonishing to them, but also quite believable. Jacob's own

skepticism was muted by the simple assent of his own flesh and blood.

Then Ruben did something quite unexpected. He took a piece of bread and offered a blessing in the memory of Jesus. Then he shared the bread with the children, saying, "If you eat this, you too become part of the story, for this bread is the very body of Jesus." Jacob's youngest passed the bread wide-eyed to her father, who ate in silence. Then Ruben took his cup, spoke another longer blessing, and passed the cup to the children saying, "By drinking from this cup, you drink from the heart of Jesus who died that we might live, for this cup is an invitation to a new covenant sealed in his blood."[147]

Western church leaders took a big step away from the early church's practice when they decided only certain people—i.e., those of a certain age who'd been "confirmed"[148]—were welcome at the Lord's table.[149]

---

147   Edward Foley, *From Age to Age: How Christians Have Celebrated the Eucharist* (Collegeville, Minnesota: Liturgical Press, 2008) 35–36. Foley includes a fictional account of a Lord's Supper to illustrate the practices of each different historical era he describes. This excerpt comes from the account illustrating the New Testament era. Interestingly, he barely mentions children in the historical part of his book, which is quite comprehensive in other ways.

148   "Confirmation" is a separate sacrament, generally following a period of instruction or catechism class. The culmination of the process is "first communion." "The history of the origin of the sacrament of Confirmation is one of the most obscure chapters in the history of Christian worship." Jean Danielou, *The Bible and the Liturgy*, first paperback English edition (Notre Dame, Indiana: University of Notre Dame Press, 1966), 114.

149   I single out Western church leaders because Eastern Orthodox churches include children in communion once they're baptized as infants. Here's one historical account of how this change happened: "Withholding communion from infants was not a reasoned decision but the result of efforts to protect the eucharistic elements from desecration or from superstitious uses. As early as the twelfth century in some areas infants received only the consecrated wine, for concern had arisen because infants had on occasion regurgitated the bread. In the thirteenth

Leaders began restricting the Lord's Supper to members, and excluding inquirers.

There's certainly no direction in the Bible that would restrict children from receiving the Lord's Supper because they're children. Someone might say a child shouldn't receive it because they haven't "decided for Christ" yet. Such an approach says they are outside the family of God, the body of Christ, because they haven't yet reached a level of mental maturity. Yet what was Jesus' attitude?

> Then children were brought to him that he might lay his hands on them and pray. The disciples rebuked the people, but Jesus said, "Let the little children come to me and do not hinder them, for to such belongs the kingdom of heaven."[150]

The Passover ceremony was a family event. The youngest child who can read gets to ask the key question: "What makes this day different than every other day?" Why shouldn't we see communion as a similar opportunity to involve and impart something to all ages of the family of God?

> [S]ymbols . . . are most effective when they either remind us of something we already know or invite us to question what we thought we knew. When a child asks,

---

century increased scrupulosity [obsessive concern with personal sins] led to withholding the chalice from the laity, which had the effect of excommunicating small children because they had already been denied the bread. In some areas, however, infants and small children continued to communicate until the Council of Trent [in the year 1562] declared that those lacking use of reason were under no obligation to receive the Eucharist." Don S. Armentrout and Robert Boak Slocum, eds., *An Episcopal Dictionary of the Church, A User-Friendly Reference for Episcopalians* (New York: Church Publishing Incorporated, 2000), 264.

150 Matthew 19:13–14, ESV.

"What does this mean?" it is often best [for adults] to reply, "What do you think it means?" and to seriously listen to the answer. For, in a child's eyes, believing is seeing. Most adults could well be reminded of that from time to time.[151]

---

151   Canon Edward N. West, *Outward Signs—The Language of Christian Symbolism*, (New York: Walker & Co., 1989), 86. Later he notes: "To oversimplify, symbolism does not work because 'seeing is believing' but because 'believing is seeing.'" This echoes Augustine's statement: *Crede, ut intelligas* ("Believe in order that you may understand") from Sermon 43.7, 9.

CAN COMMUNION BE DONE SOLO?

I appreciate people who have a passion for obeying the Lord. I appreciate that our current church and cultural context make taking the cup and bread by yourself seem reasonable. After all, if a pastor or church leader doesn't give it much attention or priority, we can do so on our own, right? Or, perhaps even more common are couples who share the Lord's Supper during their wedding ceremony, while everyone else looks on.

I love the heart behind both practices—but they still seem to miss the point of what Jesus is looking for: an act of group obedience in the context of our relationship with one another; everyone that's at a gathering in His name. When Jesus says, "Do this," he doesn't mean just that I eat from a loaf of bread—but that I share the loaf with other people. Imagine trying to do the entire Passover meal by yourself!

CHAPTER 12

TIMING

How frequently and how long should we obey?

"AFTER THE SAME manner also he took the cup, when he had supped, saying, 'This cup is the new testament in my blood: this do ye, as oft as ye drink it, in remembrance of me.'"[152] Another translation of this verse says, "whenever you drink it."[153]

What is Jesus expecting in terms of the frequency of sharing His supper? When is "whenever you drink it"?

One believer suggested to me that when Jesus said, "As oft as you eat this," He was referring to mealtime in general—the bread and the cup were simply the meal that evening, and we celebrate it whenever we eat a meal. At the other end of the spectrum, a Messianic Jewish writer advocated celebrating communion only once a year—when the Passover meal itself is eaten.

What did the early church practice? I certainly respect those traditions which celebrate the Lord's Supper weekly based upon this passage in Acts:

> [W]e sailed away from Philippi after the days of Unleavened Bread, and in five days we came to them at Troas,

---

152 1 Corinthians 11:25, KJV.
153 NIV.

where we stayed for seven days. On the first day of the
week, when we were gathered together to break bread,
Paul talked with them.[154]

The breaking of bread at Troas evidently took place on the first
day of every week. Of course, having the Lord's Supper weekly gives
precedence to the church in Troas over the early church in Jerusalem. They're described this way, "And day by day, attending the temple
together and breaking bread in their homes, they received their food
with glad and generous hearts, praising God and having favor with
all the people."[155] Any argument that the phrase "received their food"
means this was a shared meal different from the Lord's Supper has to
deal with Paul having "eaten" in Acts 20:11.[156] Both the day-by-day
event and the weekly happening were meals which went longer than
our slimmed-down version!

Since we have both weekly and day by day celebration as examples in
scripture, there's leeway in setting our own schedule. Then the question
becomes, can we appreciate the Lord's Supper however often we're sharing it? If it's not "fresh," the question may not be the particular schedule,
but our own hearts and focus. Going through a routine simply to obey
the Lord's command seems just like the Jewish people in Isaiah's time:
"When you come to appear before me, who has asked this of you, this
trampling of my courts? Stop bringing meaningless offerings!"[157]

In terms of the length of time devoted to sharing the cup and the
bread, is there a point where "efficiency" hurts the "efficacy" of an action?
Leaders who view the Supper as "a hole in the service," may rush the

---

154   Acts 20:6–7a, ESV. This shows the early church celebrating it more often than on
      Passover!
155   Acts 2:46–47a, ESV.
156   "And when Paul had gone up and had broken bread and eaten, he conversed with
      them a long while, until daybreak, and so departed." Acts 20:11, ESV.
157   Isaiah 1:12–13a, NIV.

celebration, and show by their body language that this action is less important than preaching or music.

In terms of timing, certainly the scheduled and planned event is the norm, but shouldn't there be a place for the spontaneous, as we gather with friends and want to bring the Lord more fully into our experience? Let's break bread and share the cup. As I see scripture, all that's required (besides the physical bread and cup and other believers) is for someone to take the initiative in honoring the Lord's presence and obeying His command to "Do this in remembrance of me."

WHERE'S THE MEAT?

A discussion about Passover and the Lord's Supper

Jew: We celebrate our deliverance with lamb and bread and wine—
no yeast of course; and no blood—that would be horrific.

Christian: We "celebrate" our deliverance, but we don't dine
I guess in the early church, the meals were terrific.
Now they're just so formal—and what happened to the meat?
Is there ever really anything at all—to eat?

Jew: For us it's quite a meal, cups and cups of wine.
We're to eat all the lamb, not break any of its bones.[158]

Christian: Funny, our cup is certainly described as blood.
And we do make sure to break our bread,
But they didn't break any bones in our lamb.[159]
Ohhh—that's where the meat is. . . .

158 Exodus 12:46.
159 John 19:33.

CHAPTER 13

DON'T WE NEED
TO RESOLVE MYSTERIES?

GEORGE PATTERSON'S EXPERIENCE captures my—dare I say, our?—mistaken thinking so well:

> I winced when a poorly educated village pastor handed a rather large, full glass to each person for Communion, with a whole tortilla, without the usual admonitions and explanations. "I'll have to straighten him out," I thought. The people slowly took small bites of the tortilla and sips from the glass. They lingered, holding the glass as though it contained priceless diamonds, eyes closed in meditation. I squirmed, fearing that it would take forever. These poor, illiterate *peasants!* Then I noticed the tears. I had never seen such a united, contrite spirit around the Lord's Table! Everyone was in rapt communion with Christ—except me. What had I missed?
>
> I returned home humbled and prayed as I looked again at what the apostles taught. Like many whose churches avoid the word "sacrament," I felt uneasy when someone expressed anything mystical; I feared that superstition would distort the ceremony instituted by Christ.

But wait! With my rationalistic background, was not the greater danger to *resist* the supernatural element? . . .

Having read many warnings of excessive mysticism in the Eucharist, I read again the apostles' warning in 1 Corinthians 11. Oh, oh. He warns against *failing* to recognize the mystery! Had I *over-reacted* against one extreme to err in the other? Was I basing my theology on fear rather than the Word of God? Was I keeping my students from "discerning the body" as 1 Corinthians 11:29–32 requires? Do we celebrate the "real presence" of the King, or his real absence?[160]

I wondered, "Discern *which* body?" The church body? The bread that, when eaten, is a participation in Christ's body? The physical body of Jesus that hung on the cross? What's the connection? Can bread be His body?

Wrong questions, all of them! Let God worry about how it all works. Define the mystery in human terms and you kill it.

I read what Paul wrote, "And is not the bread that we break a participation in the body of Christ? Because there is one loaf, we, who are many, are one body, for we all partake of the one loaf" (1 Cor. 10:16–17). There it was again—the inescapable mystery. I had taught with no qualms about God's supernatural work in uniting a couple in marriage as one flesh and its mysterious connection with the union between Christ and his church

---

160   George Patterson shared during a workshop in Kansas City, July 2014, that this phrase was spoken by another missionary challenging him on his approach: "If you want to focus on the real absence of the Lord, you can." Interestingly, Paul's words in 1 Corinthians 11:26 (NKJV) emphasize that in one way He's absent from our celebration: "For as often as you eat this bread and drink this cup, you proclaim the Lord's death *till He comes.*"

(Eph. 5:25–32). But I had failed to see—feared to see—
that Christ and his apostles taught the same mystical
union with the body of Christ in the Eucharist![161]

In a similar way, I thought I had to have the answer and resolve the mystery. Sacrament or ordinance? How precisely is it Jesus' body and blood? What happens to the bread? What is discerning the body?

Why was the apostle Paul so adamant about "discerning the body" in the Lord's Supper? The Lord allowed some to be ill and to die because they failed to discern it.[162] What "body" did Paul mean? The body of Jesus that hung on the cross? The universal Church? The body of believers that gathered in Corinth to break bread? Human reason clamors for a simple explanation, that the "body" be one or the other; but God's Word doesn't use language that way. The context of Paul's remarks about the bread and wine, including 1 Corinthians 10:16–17, shows that he was probably thinking about all three aspects of Jesus' body.[163]

Of course, many have grappled with questions like these over the centuries. Because they've come to different answers, this action to demonstrate our unity (that we are "one loaf") is now a key point of division. I've had the experience of being excluded from receiving the Lord's Supper in several different settings: one time because that body, from a Plymouth Brethren tradition, only served it to people they had known for quite some time *and* whose statement of beliefs agreed with the leaders' beliefs; other times, because among Roman Catholic or Eastern Orthodox, participants must either be baptized into that tradition or agree to a particular statement of understanding about what happens in the Lord's Supper.

---

161 George Patterson and Bob Scroggins, *Church Multiplication Guide,* revised edition (Pasadena, California: William Carey Library, 2002), 74. Used by permission.
162 1 Corinthians 11:27–34.
163 Patrick O'Connor, *Reproducible Pastoral Training* (Pasadena, California: William Carey Library. 2006), 64.

How did I feel when turned away from the Table? I certainly didn't feel like I was hearing my Master invite me to come and drink of Him! I couldn't have described the body's attitude as hospitable. There was nothing welcoming to me about being told I couldn't participate in sharing the cup and the bread!

I can appreciate groups and leaders turn people away from the table in order to defend the truth, or prevent blasphemy or desecration of the Lord's Supper. But do we need to defend the truth in that way?

Alexander Solzhenitsyn said in a different context, but it applies: "One word of truth outweighs the world." Or to put it another, way, whatever happens in a Lord's Supper—doesn't it simply happen? Can we say that the effects of the Supper in us, or the participation in His blood and body, would somehow be limited by the credentials of another participant? Or particular attitudes the participant has? Or even the condition of the server's heart?[164]

If our heart is to obey the Lord and bring His presence to mind and the Lord desires that very thing as well—how can someone else interfere? Now the Lord's Supper is a group action, so other individuals' actions and attitudes could conceivably limit the overall group experience. But ultimately it's a group action with our Lord; He's the major player!

God's truth, expressed by God, in accord with His promises, is "bigger" than us. He will overcome our mental reservations and supersede our opinions and hesitations. He will partner and participate with whoever desires whenever our hearts take a step toward Him.

---

164   As author John Sandford put it in a personal note: "The sacrament is valid despite the condition of the priest."

CHAPTER 14

CON OR NON, TRANS UP OR DOWN?

What did Jesus mean: "This is my body"?

ALTHOUGH GEORGE PATTERSON warned us against trying to resolve the mystery, many have attempted it. This becomes most acute in terms of trying to describe what happens to the bread and the cup. There are several different schools of thought.

Transubstantiation says that once the bread and the cup are blessed they become only the actual physical body and blood of Jesus and still retain the appearance of bread and wine. The closest I could think of as an analogy for transubstantiation would be handing someone a generic CD-R I just burned music onto and saying, "Now you've got the Beatles." (I had been really quite pleased with this analogy.) The CD certainly has the same physical appearance, but it has been permanently and completely changed. However, Father Dennis of the Benedictine Monastery in Atchison, Kansas, pointed out to me what he regards as a weakness in the analogy: You don't have the Beatles themselves—just their music. He said transubstantiation would result in George, John, Paul, and Ringo stepping out of the CD! His elaboration of my analogy shows the difficulty of describing the bread as the literal body of Jesus—does Jesus step out of the bread? How does the bread being His flesh relate to Jesus, evidently in bodily form, sitting at the right hand of the throne of God in heaven?

Transubstantiation is the Roman Catholic position. Another "trans" is the Eastern Orthodox position: *transelementation*. What's the difference?

A key difference would be to picture transubstantiation as Jesus "descending" into the bread and cup, while in transelementation the cup and bread "ascend" into His presence in heaven. Rather than having something replace the objects' qualities as bread and cup, those qualities are absorbed into something greater. "Transubstantiation asserts that the body of Christ is enclosed in the consecrated bread; transelementation, that Christ by His Spirit assimilates the consecrated bread to his life-giving flesh so that it becomes one with the bread by which it is imparted."[165]

Consubstantiation sees the bread and the cup as taking on the actual spiritual presence of Jesus. This would historically be the understanding of many Lutherans. To me, "consubstantiation" is similar to a light bulb. The bulb is "on" or "off," depending upon whether electricity is flowing through it. One writer from years ago used a slightly different analogy: "even as His Divine nature is in the human as warmth is in the iron."[166] Heat has an interesting nuance compared to most electric light bulbs—the temperature of a hot iron can vary. We can certainly feel Jesus' presence as being different levels of intensity—is it in reality?[167]

The *non-substantial*[168] view sees the bread and the cup like a picture. Jesus' words, "This is my body," would be like gesturing at a photograph: "That's my child."

I've viewed the argument as a distraction—but is it? Our understanding can affect our practice. Lou Engle, founder of "The Call" prayer movement, maintains that the lack of respect for the Lord's Supper in many Protestant churches stems directly from not seeing the Lord as truly present in the bread and cup.

---

165 George Hunsinger, *The Eucharist and Ecumenism: Let Us Keep the Feast* (Cambridge, United Kingdom: Cambridge Press, 2008), 74–75.

166 Martin Luther, quoted in Henry E. Dosker, "Lord's Supper," *International Standard Bible Encyclopedia* (Grand Rapids, Michigan: Wm. B. Eerdmans Publishing, 1974 reprint of 1956 edition), 1926.

167 The heat in iron analogy has also been used to describe the transelementation view.

168 Yes, that's my cute term to fit with the other prefixes!

Let's look at the Last Supper as a test for the different views. What did the disciples understand that night?

To start with, consider this question: did the Lord eat Himself?

There are some who maintain the Lord didn't actually partake Himself. This thinking led many Lutheran churches during past centuries to require a solo pastor leading a communion service to abstain from the cup and the bread. This was because his leadership role was seen as similar to Jesus' at the Last Supper.[169] The gospel accounts say Jesus served His disciples and the accounts don't mention Him eating, but saying Jesus didn't eat the bread he spoke over or drink the cup He described as His blood, stretch the text too far. After all, Jesus said He was eager to eat the meal—not simply share the time with them. The account in Mark does say about the cup:

> And He (Jesus) took a cup, and when He had given thanks He gave it to them, and they all drank of it. And He said to them, "This is my blood of the covenant, which is poured out for many. Truly, I say to you, I will not drink again of the fruit of the vine until that day when I drink it anew in the kingdom of God."[170]

One can argue "all" is ambiguous, since it could apply just to the disciples. But the statement "I will not drink again" is in both Matthew and Mark, and implies He's drinking it with them at that time.

So why is resolving this important for our understanding of how Jesus is present in the supper?

That question never occurred to me until my friend Nina Robnett pointed out: Jesus, at the Last Supper, seems to be saying that He was eating His own body and drinking His own blood.

---

169   Toivo Harjunpaa, "The Pastor's Communion," *Concordia Theological Quarterly*, Volume 52, Numbers 2–3 (April–July 1988): 149ff.

170   Mark 14:23–25, ESV.

That certainly can affect our understanding of what He was saying! Clearly, at that moment, His disciples could see that the bread was separate and distinct from His flesh, His physical body. He wasn't bleeding into the cup. Each of the disciples would have interpreted what happened that night in terms of what Jesus said months earlier, as reported in John 6. (I will explore this idea further in the Afterthought section of this book.)

In addition, Paul's directions on conducting the Lord's Supper describe the bread as Jesus' body, and then within the next chapter Paul describes Jesus' followers as His body. Could it be that Jesus is saying that *the action of His followers sharing the bread* constitutes "This is My body"? In other words, not bread as an object, but our action of coming together and sharing the bread is "His body?" (Is the Lord's Supper a verb more than a noun? We'll examine that question in the next section.)

Paul ties together the body of Christ as people and the body of Christ as bread: "The bread that we break, is it not a participation in the body of Christ? Because there is one bread, we who are many are one body, for we all partake of the one bread."[171] How can Jesus have a body that's made up of people, apparently connected only in a spiritual and social sense; and yet describe the action of them eating bread as "His body?" By eating together, Jesus was establishing a corporate oneness with His disciples, something beyond just the spiritual and social dimensions. When this corporate oneness was broken by the disciples' desertion after His arrest, He reestablished it and communicated His forgiveness by eating with them again after His resurrection.

One way to picture the Last Supper is to think of a Mobius strip. If you have a strip of paper it has two sides, and four edges. Yet once you twist one end and attach it to the other, you've suddenly changed it to have only one side and one edge. Two distinct sides have become one. We could even see his action at the Last Supper like forming a Mobius strip—Jesus' body eating itself. It brings to mind Paul's words: "God was in Christ

---

171   1 Corinthians 11:16b–17a, ESV.

reconciling the world to Himself." Can we say that Jesus, in his humanity, was eating and drinking God's spiritual presence at the Last Supper?

A different approach to explaining what happens comes from a Christian thinker from India, A. J. Appasamy. Robin Boyd sets the context for his comments:

> Rather than going into the controversies of western sac-ramental theology with their discussion of the real pres-ence, transubstantiation, "in, with and under" and so on, Appasamy turns to the [Hindu thinker] Rāmānuja's idea that all created beings are "the body of God." . . . So Jesus takes the created elements of bread and wine as the instruments for fulfilling his purpose:
>
> "They were to reveal to men His utter love for them leading to the complete sacrifice of Himself on the Cross. . . . The bread and wine were to become a new body of our Lord. In tasting them we taste His love. . . . Truly the bread and wine become the body and blood of our Lord because through them He fulfils His end of making known His love to men and gathering them into the intimacy and closeness of fellowship with Him."
>
> It is an impressive interpretation. There is no men-tion of substance and accident, nor even of sign and symbol. Yet God chooses and uses *this* "body," of bread and wine, and in receiving it we receive the "Spirit" behind it, Christ Himself.[172]

---

172   Robin Boyd, *An Introduction to Indian Christian Theology* (Delhi, India: Indian Society for Promoting Christian Knowledge, 1969), 139–140, quoting A. J. Appasamy, *The Gospel and India's Heritage* (London: SPCK, 1942), 208.

WHAT'S UNITY LIKE?

Getting leaders (generally not normal believers!) to agree on how to understand what happens as we share the Lord's Supper is a problem. British church leader Nicky Gumbel's experience gives one picture of the problem:

And it was fascinating to me what happened when the Catholic churches started running [The Alpha Course], because what happened was this: if I'm really honest, when we put together this material, *Questions of Life*, we weren't thinking the Catholic churches would be running Alpha—we were thinking that maybe Methodist, Baptist might be, but it never occurred to me, if I'm honest, that Catholic churches would be at that stage.

But shortly after we produced this, I met a Catholic man who said to me: "There is nothing in this that we disagree with." He said, "There are things we'd want to *add*—but that's true of every part of the church: you can't teach the entire Christian faith in fifteen sessions." Then I had lunch with a Catholic theologian. And this Catholic theologian said: "That's absolutely right, there's nothing in here that we as Catholics disagree with." He said, "There is one word it would help us if you could change. It's where you say the bread and the wine represent the body and blood of Christ." He said, "We don't actually disagree with that, it's just that it would help us if you could change it."

So I thought, "Well, what do we do?" And that week I was doing a conference in Wales at the invitation of the then Bishop of Monmouth, Bishop Rowan Williams, now the Archbishop of Wales, who comes from the Liberal Catholic wing of the Church of England. And he was very keen on Alpha, he had ordered all his clergy to attend this conference. We said, you know, "We'd like them to come voluntarily": "No, no, no, far too important!" Bishop Rowan Williams was Regis Professor of Divinity at Oxford University at the age of 36. Brilliant theologian, very involved in ecumenical discussions around the world.

So I went to him at the first lunch break of the conference, and I said, "Bishop Rowan, could you help us?" I showed him the section on the sacraments in here, and I said, "The Catholics say this word 'represent'—it's not that they disagree with it, but it would help them if we could change it. But," I said, "I'm also very conscious that the Presbyterians in Northern Ireland are running Alpha, and they probably feel equally strongly but possibly in a slightly different direction. Is there a word that we could use that would be acceptable to the Catholics and to the Protestants?"

And he looked at [me] and he said, "If you can find the word, you will get the Nobel Peace Prize!" He said, "My advice to you is leave it exactly as it is, and I think you'll find that everyone can work with it." And that's what we've done, and we've found that everyone—that the people have been able to work with it.[173]

Will the "unity of faith" which Ephesians speaks of involve unity of practice?[174] Is it possible that the Holy Spirit will simply bless one particular practice, or understanding, of the Lord's Supper and that will become the consensus? Some might agree with what C. S. Lewis said:

The very last thing I want to do is to unsettle in the mind of any Christian, whatever his denomination, the concepts—for him traditional—by which he finds it profitable to represent to himself what is happening when he receives the bread and wine. I could wish that

173 Nicky Gumbel. Transcript of a training talk: "The Practicalities of Alpha," circa 2003 given at Holy Trinity Brompton, London, England. Copyright Nicky Gumbel; used by permission.
174 Ephesians 4:13.

no definitions had ever been felt to be necessary; and still more that none had been allowed to make divisions between churches.[175]

As a young believer, I went on a field trip with my seminary class. We visited a grade school of a tradition that practices "closed" communion—that is, only members of their particular group are allowed to participate. I had only the haziest awareness of such things, but I was quite struck at the end of our visit when the school's principal insisted with great excitement on sharing the Lord's Supper with us. I could sense something important was taking place—but I didn't have a grid for understanding what it was. Looking back, I appreciate the courage of that headmaster, to invite all of us Jesus followers to take part—even if we weren't members of his tradition! Hurray—may this be repeated many times in coming years.

Instead of looking for a common description, or mental understanding, let's begin simply "doing this," sharing the Lord's Supper with one another, and trust Him to work out the rest! Or, to put it another way, shouldn't we be more focused on what's happening to us, rather than what's happening to the bread?

After all, isn't the mystery of why what is happening to us doesn't match what the New Testament says *should* happen among believers the more important mystery?

---

175 Lewis, *Letters to Malcolm,* 101–102. Of course, Lewis goes on to say something which might appear to hint at a point of view: "I do not know and can't imagine what the disciples understood our Lord to mean when, His body still unbroken and His blood unshed, He handed them the bread and wine saying *they* were His body and blood." See the *Afterthought* later in this book, for my view of what the disciples understood.

CHAPTER 15

NOUN AND VERB TOGETHER

WHAT IS THE LORD'S SUPPER? If you look at a cup of grape juice and a piece of bread are you seeing the Lord's Supper?

Do you think of communion as a "thing"—or an "action"?

To me, the Lord's Supper is something that happens—not a place or a thing. Our Lord said, "Do this in remembrance of me," which means there have to be people involved who are connecting with Him and with each other. "Do" is, of course, a verb—an action, not a noun.[176] Grape juice and bread without the actions of faith, sharing, eating, and calling to mind (remembering) are just grape juice and bread.

The traditional definition of a noun is an "idea, person, place, or thing." Is the Lord's Supper a noun because the presence of Jesus makes it a person? Can you call the Lord's Supper a thing? Any resolution to the question, "What happens to the elements in the Lord's Supper?" must include the obvious requirement for the Lord's Supper to take place as a group action. There has to be a gathering in faith and a recognition of what's involved in the action of breaking bread or drinking the cup.

"Body" of course is a noun—a thing, an object we can sense. But Paul refers to a body of Christ as a collection, a gathering of human beings, and to bread that is broken and shared. There's motion and action in

---

176 The "this" phrases "This is my body" and "Do this in remembrance of me" are so close together. Is it possible we should see "this is my body" as pointing to the action of being together and taking the bread—not just to the bread as an object?

references like this one describing people joined together in the body of Christ: "from whom the whole body, joined and knit together by what every joint supplies, according to the effective working by which every part does its share, causes growth of the body for the edifying of itself in love."[177]

When our Lord said, "This is my body" as He broke and shared the bread, isn't it possible He was referring as much to the action and context as the object? This understanding can revolutionize the centuries-old debate we discussed a few pages back.

> God is easier to get our minds, concepts, and theology around if the Godhead remains only noun.
>
> Nouns provide certainty, identity. Position. Stability. Nouns supply the answer to "What?" . . . Nouns minimize relational action. Nouns rein verbs' constant movement, constant activity. . . . Verbs tell the story. For life's complex and confusing conundrums, we need verbs, not nouns.
>
> Verbs describe an ongoing process. Human beings, for example, become. . . . A snapshot of a person is not who they are; it is only a representation of a minute part of what they may be at a specific moment.
>
> Plus, we are in a constant state of *relating.* However, when viewed as an objective noun we are treated as inanimate—without personality, individuality, and growth.
>
> Nouns may be neat, may be hygienic, but also may fail to deliver. . . . God describes himself with the verb "I am." The Trinity is not three objects. The Trinity is a dance of three verbs. Three "I ams."[178]

---

177 Ephesians 3:16, NKJV.
178 Joseph Myers, *Organic Community,* (Grand Rapids, Michigan: Baker Books, 2007), 152.

As we're remembering Him, let's take this point one step further. The apostle John makes the simple statement: "God is love."[179] Is love a noun or a verb? An idea or an action? "Idea" seems like a pretty weak description of the type of word "love" is. Doesn't "love" transcend that category? The very grammar and structure of our language can limit our understanding of our God. God, in His nature, is both action and person, verb and noun. We enlarge our relationship when we can think in bigger, growing ways about who He is. His Supper highlights that.

179   1 John 4:8, 16.

CHAPTER 16

WHY THE CURRENT APPROACH?

AFTER ALL I'VE SAID as a case for changing our practice of the Lord's Supper—is there a case for the present practice?

Defense No. 1: "Our Lord is sovereign in church history."

One argument is that the way things are is the way they should be, because the Lord is sovereign over church history.

Is the Lord sovereign over church history?

Of course, at one level, yes. The assumption that God directs human destiny and activity can be so much of a given that we don't think through how it works out in practice. Still, on occasion we may find ourselves wondering how humans can be responsible for their choices and God still be sovereign. This question seems particularly acute in one area we'd think would be under His most specific direction: church activities and practices. We know, as individuals, that we can act and think in ways which aren't our Lord's desire. We can see aspects of our life together, our life "in church," that aren't His desire. Is it possible He desires something more for us in the way we share His Supper?

Some see our practice of the Lord's Supper as becoming refined over the years.[180] I trust it's obvious by now I'd use different verbs! To me, our practice has become distorted and diluted.

180　For instance, see Keith Watkins' comments in Appendix 2, in the section "Celebrating Communion in a Meal."

Some branches of the body of Christ have died out over time. Evidently our Lord didn't want to allow Arians or Marcionites to continue, for instance. Yet there's still a wide variety of both thinking and practice among those who claim Jesus' name! Our Lord is surely, and accurately described, as patient. He appears to be content to work slowly in bringing us to what we'd see as "unity of faith."

As we look specifically at the Lord's Supper, we see God in His sovereignty has allowed a situation where "In sacramental churches preaching atrophies; in preaching churches the sacraments are secondary. . . . No Church has been able to achieve in practice the equality to which it in theory holds. As the one increases the other decreases."[181] But is that our Lord's desire? Or is He allowing us humans to seek Him in different ways until . . . ?

We can look for something spiritually fuller and deeper in our celebrations of the Lord's Supper[182]—not just because of the questions we've examined here, but because there's promise of something more to come in Scripture. Paul prophesies a day that's coming:

> Again I ask: Did [the people of Israel] stumble so as to fall beyond recovery? Not at all! Rather, because of their transgression, salvation has come to the Gentiles to make Israel envious. But if their transgression means riches for the world, and their loss means riches for the Gentiles, how much greater riches will their full inclusion bring![183]

181   Leonard Verduin, *The Reformers and Their Stepchildren*, (Sarasota, Florida: Pinecraft Publishers, 1991 reprint of 1964 edition by Eerdmans),136.
182   What could "fuller and deeper" be like? See the opening story, "Could This Fantasy Become Real?"; chapter 8, "Increasing Expectancy"; the story after the Postscript, "Finding Home"; and the suggestions in appendices 2, 3 and 4.
183   Romans 11:11–12, NLT.

As the number of believers of Jewish ethnicity increases, we will begin to see what "much greater riches" means. One thing it could mean is that churches will develop that have dynamic celebrations of our Lord's Supper *and* dynamic preaching. That seems to me to be a dream on our Lord's heart.

What is, isn't necessarily what should be. At one point, I worked with a pastor who was fascinated by the question, "What's the bare minimum we need to be church? To do church?" He was pursuing something that could be called "simple church." Simplicity is one key to focusing on and following our Lord. But there's a weakness in this "minimalist" approach pointed out by the counter-question, "Why not pursue the most we can have when we do church?"[184]

What is the most we can have in our actual experience of church? This brings to mind phrases like "God's best" or "God's standard." But those can be tricky terms. By those terms we can set ourselves up for failure and condemnation. Don't we need to start thinking about what God has available for us based on His glorious acceptance of us—just where we are?

Yet there's no valid reason to settle for less when God's Word holds out promises of more. Practices of church bodies have changed throughout the ages. If it's possible that those haven't always been positive changes, then let's recover what's lost. Or if it's possible that the church has never entered into all that the Lord provides, let's press on. The action of the Lord's Supper can be more glorious than we've ever experienced.

Defense No. 2: Paul said to eat at home

How can I suggest that we expand our practice of the Lord's Supper, when Paul himself seems to endorse making it bare-bones? Let's look at what he said:

---

184 My thanks to Adam Cox, team leader (lead pastor) of Navah Church in urban Kansas City, Missouri, for pointing this out to me.

When you come together, it is not the Lord's supper that you eat. For in eating, each one goes ahead with his own meal. One goes hungry, another gets drunk. What! Do you not have houses to eat and drink in? Or do you despise the church of God and humiliate those who have nothing? What shall I say to you? Shall I commend you in this? No, I will not.[185]

He goes on to conclude his correction of the Corinthian church, "So then, my brothers, when you come together to eat, wait for [or share with] one another—if anyone is hungry, let him eat at home—so that when you come together it will not be for judgment."[186]

Wait—wait! Does Paul want to leave the people with nothing—with nothing? Evidently in the Corinthian gatherings there were hungry but well-off people who were bringing food and eating it right away, while the needy were coming late without any food—and leaving without being fed.

Wasn't Paul's point that those who have something should be providing for others? In his conclusion, in which he's addressing those who couldn't wait for others—he's not saying we shouldn't have a meal together, but that we need to be courteous and generous.

As I wrestle again and again with the question: "Why are we doing communion the way most church bodies do?" the defenses of the current approach seem flimsy. Perhaps it's mainly a case of the urgent crowding the important out of minds. Human needs, whether individual or group, keep our mind from focusing on: What does our Lord deserve? What is He looking for in our celebrations remembering Him?

---

185   1 Corinthians 11:20–22, ESV.
186   1 Corinthians 11:33–34, ESV. "Share with" is the alternate rendering given in the ESV.

LOOKING AT JOHN 6

THE SHOCK AND HORROR of what happened then is no doubt incomprehensible to us. We don't have the mental framework to begin to understand what offended these first-century Israelites.

A wonderful miracle-working teacher had aroused much hope. People were thinking, "Perhaps we're going to throw off Roman rule after all!" But now this teacher was saying outlandish things, which at a minimum, seemed to violate God's commands. He said they could have no part of Him unless they repudiated their traditions, and He seemed to call upon them to stoop to the level of pagans—those idol worshipers and demon sympathizers! Let's take some moments to actually read the Bible's account and see what happened when Jesus multiplied bread to feed a crowd:[187]

> Yeshua took the loaves, gave thanks, and distributed them to the people who were sitting there. He did the same thing with the fish. All the people ate as much as they wanted.
>
> When the people were full, Yeshua told his disciples, "Gather the leftover pieces so that nothing will be wasted."

---

187 I know I take some risk in asking you to read a long Bible text, but we need to in order to discuss it well. I've used a translation that isn't widely used, to help us look at it with fresh eyes.

The disciples gathered the leftover pieces of bread and filled twelve baskets. When the people saw the miracle Yeshua performed, they said, "This man is certainly the prophet who is to come into the world." Yeshua realized that the people intended to take him by force and make him king.. . . .

[That night Jesus walks across the stormy sea of Galilee, joins up with his terrified disciples on their boat, and calms the storm with a couple of words. The next morning the crowd eventually catches up with him.]

The people asked Yeshua, "What does God want us to do?" Yeshua replied to them, "God wants to do something for you so that you believe in the one whom he has sent." The people asked him, "What miracle are you going to perform so that we can see it and believe in you? What are you going to do? Our ancestors ate the manna in the desert. Scripture says, 'He gave them bread from heaven to eat.'"[188]

Yeshua said to them, "I can guarantee this truth: Moses didn't give you bread from heaven, but my Father gives you the true bread from heaven. God's bread is the man who comes from heaven and gives life to the world." They said to him, "Sir, give us this bread all the time." Yeshua told them, "I am the bread of life. Whoever comes to me will never become hungry, and whoever believes in me will never become thirsty.". . . The Jews began to criticize Yeshua for saying, "I am the bread that came from heaven." They asked, "Isn't this man Yeshua, Joseph's

---

188   The crowd was looking for a Messiah who would be identified in part by the miraculous provision of bread—now, ironically, they miss the confirmation that Jesus is the Messiah because of the "ordinary" bread He miraculously provides them.

son? Don't we know his father and mother? How can he say now, 'I came from heaven'?" Yeshua responded, "Stop criticizing me! People cannot come to me unless the Father who sent me brings them to me. I will bring these people back to life on the last day.. . . . I am the bread of life. Your ancestors ate the manna in the desert and died. This is the bread that comes from heaven so that whoever eats it won't die. I am the living bread that came from heaven. Whoever eats this bread will live forever. The bread I will give to bring life to the world is my flesh." The Jews began to quarrel with each other. They said, "How can this man give us his flesh to eat?" Yeshua told them, "I can guarantee this truth: If you don't eat the flesh of the Son of Man and drink his blood, you don't have the source of life in you. Those who eat my flesh and drink my blood have eternal life, and I will bring them back to life on the last day. My flesh is true food, and my blood is true drink. Those who eat my flesh and drink my blood live in me, and I live in them. The Father who has life sent me, and I live because of the Father. So those who feed on me will live because of me. This is the bread that came from heaven. It is not like the bread your ancestors ate. They eventually died. Those who eat this bread will live forever." Yeshua said this while he was teaching in a synagogue in Capernaum. When many of Yeshua's disciples heard him, they said, "What he says is hard to accept. Who wants to listen to him anymore?". . . . Yeshua's speech made many of his disciples go back to the lives they had led before they followed Yeshua. [189]

189   John 6:11–15a, 28–35, 41–44, 48–60, 66, GOD'S WORD. From the "Names of God" version of this translation, so Jesus is rendered Yeshua.

The offense of the hearers is important in interpreting Jesus' words. Certainly part of "eating Jesus' flesh" is coming to Him and believing in Him (John 6:35), but, narrowly defined, that wouldn't offend people who were already following him. Jesus' boldness in using "I am" about Himself, when "I am" is also the name of God, may have contributed to the fierce reaction. Still, the meaning of Jesus' claims must be bigger—much bigger—to offend them. Imagine this God-man saying, in our day, with perfect calm in His voice, "Drink me!" We might be mystified, but probably not to the point of offense.

Jesus didn't immediately cut off a finger and offer his disciples a cannibalistic *hors d'oeurve* or a cup of blood! Nor did He do anything similar later.

His specific instructions didn't come until the Last Supper. The twelve disciples who were part of that Last Supper would have understood what Jesus said to them that night based on all that He'd said earlier—like what he said here in John 6. Whether Jesus said it thirty-six months before or only a few months before, clearly the words made a deep impression. The apostle John remembered them years later when he wrote down his gospel.

Some of the disciples at that supper may have had a flash, "Oh, *this* is what Jesus meant!" The penny was dropping into place.[190]

So back to John 6: Why was Jesus' audience so offended? Because it sounded cannibalistic or masochistic, or did they just think He was talking crazy? Or, if they were trying to think metaphorically, were they just so mystified they became angry? Or: Were His would-be followers being challenged at a more personal level?

Let me suggest that part of the reason for their anger could be in an instruction given to Moses:

---

190   If we believe Jesus actually said those words when John says He did, wouldn't they be the interpretive framework His disciples would use when they heard His words at the Last Supper?

As for anyone, whether of the house of Israel or of the aliens residing among them, who consumes any blood, I will set myself against that individual and will cut that person off from among the people, since the life of the flesh is in the blood, and I have given it to you to make atonement on the altar for yourselves, because it is the blood as life that makes atonement.[191]

At a basic level, Jesus' listeners knew they were forbidden to eat any blood—this practice made them different from other people.

The seriousness to the Jewish people of this prohibition against eating blood is shown by the Jerusalem Council described in Acts 15. When the Jerusalem church, elders, and apostles met to decide how to bring Gentile believers into relationship with Jewish believers, the early church ended up insisting on only a few basic requirements: "You must abstain from eating food offered to idols, from consuming blood or the meat of strangled animals, and from sexual immorality."[192]

A whole plethora of God's instructions and Jewish cultural traditions didn't make the list (such as, most notably, the practice of circumcision). But Gentile believers were asked in the strongest possible terms to not eat blood!

Most interpret this list as operational instructions—how people from two different cultures can get along as they're joined together into one body. It isn't a new revision of the Torah. Stealing isn't made acceptable because it isn't on the list. No, these instructions help one culture respect another. It shows how important the prohibition on imbibing blood was to the Jews who heard Jesus' challenge.

Jesus' words in John 6 cut across the grain of his culture—and offended so deeply that many would-be followers turned away.

---

191   Leviticus 17:10–11, NABre.
192   Acts 15:29, NLT.

POSTSCRIPT AND SUMMARY

I COULD FOLLOW JESUS in my culture and not even give much attention or thought to the Lord's Supper, partly because of my understanding of symbols. After all, symbols don't have any power beyond what I give them, right? And they're mostly used to manipulate, not to convey truth or impart life—right?

No, symbols can convey meaning and power—a flag conveys more than simply being colored cloth.

Likewise, isn't it possible that there's something more available for us in the Lord's Supper? Could we enjoy what the New Testament church enjoyed when they gathered to feast on, and with, our Lord?

I'm interested in individuals and groups discovering for themselves how to apply the principles I've highlighted. The appendices have some specific suggestions for those who ask "Where should we start?" Still, any focus on methods may miss something. As I have pondered the words in the books of Acts, "And they devoted themselves to the apostles' teaching and the fellowship, to the breaking of bread and the prayers,"[193] I have come to see these words may be more "descriptive" than "prescriptive." When the life of Jesus flows in a group—their fellowship sooner or later will involve food. It's inevitable.

Can you seek the Lord with me for a transformation in our group experience of His Supper? I sense that the experience of many separate, individual mini-transactions with the Lord in our current ceremony of

---

193 Acts 2:42, ESV.

communion doesn't match the experience of partnership and fellowship which the early church enjoyed. Let's close with a description of what this could have looked like.

FINDING HOME

I rushed down the narrow lane from my master's house to the broader thoroughfare that took me to the nice part of Phillipi. I knew things would have gotten started, but I was hoping I'd still make it in time for honoring our Lord—not Caesar, but Jesus.

Only a few weeks before, a fellow tutor, who was also a slave, had talked to me at the marketplace about this new message. I was always paying attention to new messages, but this one was *really* different. I could tell because there was a hope in Joseph's eyes, in his voice, that I hadn't seen before. I didn't know him well—we worked in different households—but I trusted there was something worth investigating about this message. It was a message that someone, a real person, had conquered death and offered that hope to all of us!

I was still thinking through all the implications of his startling message, but this I knew—I was committed to it. I'd gotten bathed in water on my last day off as a first step in obeying this new message, along with several of the others from this new way.

Now it was the first day of the week, time for our regular feast. Of course, I couldn't bring anything. The thought of taking food from my master's kitchen was out of the question. But in the spirit of this new message there were those who brought extra food to the gathering.

We were meeting at a rich merchant's home—her name was Lydia. She had a large inner courtyard where we gathered. The weekly gathering had obviously been going for some time when I joined, and they had a system of everyone serving the food to themselves. It was hard for me to adapt to—I was so used to being the one serving and then grabbing my food in the back portico. But evidently, Lydia, and Joseph, who did some of the speaking, had thought it through and wanted to make clear we were all cared for by the God who raised Jesus from the dead.

Tonight, by the time I got there, everyone else had almost finished eating. Even for a slave, I had long hours and tonight had been longer than usual. Still, I was grateful there was some bread and porridge available. I knew Joseph would have already blessed the bread. He'd say Hebrew words over it, words I didn't understand but they had a wonderful poetic flow to them. Then Lydia would hold the bread up, so all could see, and break that loaf in two. She'd say in Greek so we all understood: "Our Lord Jesus took bread on the night he was betrayed, broke it, and said this is my body—given for you!"

I'm guessing no one would say anything at that point for at least five minutes, as the bread was passed and people took a piece and began to eat. No one was in a rush.

Tonight it looked like there had been some figs for the people who got there early, as well as another kind of porridge besides the one I'd gotten. But I was content—I munched on the bread and porridge and looked at what was becoming a new household, a new family, for me. A family where I was told my worth came from God—not my status as a tutor or the family name I slaved for.

I was glad I'd gotten there before the end of the eating, because my heart looked forward to hearing Joseph say: "We take this cup, as the cup of the Lord. When He died, He gave us eternal life and cleared away all the shame, guilt, and fear of our hearts. That's our inheritance—and it's all included as we drink this cup."

Tonight was no different, and as the wine coursed down my throat I felt a warmth that went beyond the physical: I was home. As I looked across the courtyard and connected with a few others' eyes, I had to check myself and make sure this was real. Because when I thought more about it, I wasn't sure I'd ever known "home" like this. I grew up as the son of a slave—so I could tell now, as an adult, that my upbringing had been restricted. And I was wise enough, at least I told myself I was, that I could realize there were some things I didn't know! But this I did know—an ultimate personal being, a God beyond gods, had touched me and changed me.

Tonight my thoughts were interrupted, a little suddenly I thought, by Andronicus. He obviously had approval from Lydia and Joseph: "Tonight, we're going to sing together, a song praising our Lord. We'll repeat the Hebrew word 'Hallelujah' like this"—and he proceeded to demonstrate and then we joined in.

Several years later, when a scroll about Jesus' life, written down by one of Paul's team, a doctor named Luke, arrived in Philippi, I learned that's what happened after that last meal Jesus had with His close followers: They sang a song and left that room—to go to the place where He was arrested.

WHY OFFER COMMUNION TO EVERYONE AT A GATHERING?

1. *Because as a form of proclaiming the Lord's death, we want to make clear everyone is invited to trust and know Him:*
   - "For as often as you eat this bread and drink the cup, you proclaim the Lord's death until he comes" (1 Corinthians 11:26, ESV).
   - The Good News is available for everyone to respond to! "For I am not ashamed of this Good News about Christ. It is the power of God at work, saving everyone who believes—the Jew first and also the Gentile" (Romans 1:16, NLT).

2. *Because any effort to "fence" our Lord's table, (for leaders to give qualifications one has to meet to participate), can end up sending the wrong message:*
   - The effect could be similar to a situation James addresses: "My dear brothers and sisters, how can you claim to have faith in our glorious Lord Jesus Christ if you favor some people over others? For example, suppose someone comes into your meeting dressed in fancy clothes and expensive jewelry, and another comes in who is poor and dressed in dirty clothes. If you give special attention and a good seat to the rich person, but you say to the poor one, 'You can stand over there, or else sit on the floor'—well, doesn't this discrimination show that your judgments are guided by evil motives?" (James 2:1–4, NLT).

3. *Because Paul's warning on how people participate in the Lord's Supper in an unworthy manner is actually focused on ensuring that everyone can be a part:*

    - "When you meet together, you are not really interested in the Lord's Supper. For some of you hurry to eat your own meal without sharing with others. As a result, some go hungry while others get drunk. What? Don't you have your own homes for eating and drinking? Or do you really want to disgrace God's church and shame the poor? What am I supposed to say? Do you want me to praise you? Well, I certainly will not praise you for this!. . . . So, my dear brothers and sisters, when you gather for the Lord's Supper, wait for each other. If you are really hungry, eat at home so you won't bring judgment upon yourselves when you meet together. I'll give you instructions about the other matters after I arrive" (1 Corinthians 11:20–22, 33–34a, NLT).
    - Certainly the issue Paul was concerned about—of common courtesy and waiting so everyone can participate—isn't an issue today in nearly all churches.

4. *Because we don't want to hinder anyone obeying our Lord's commands, including children:*

    - Jesus' attitude was one of including people—and children. "Woe to you, scholars of the law! You have taken away the key of knowledge. You yourselves did not enter and you stopped those trying to enter" (Luke 11:52, NABre).
    - "But Jesus called them unto him, and said, Suffer little children to come unto me, and forbid them not: for of such is the kingdom of God" (Luke 18:16, KJV).

5. *Because the instruction to examine ourselves before participating in our Lord's Supper has been misunderstood:*

- We don't need to meet a performance standard before participating. Unfortunately, many translations of 1 Corinthians 11:28 use the phrase "examine ourselves," which can lead to an inward focus looking to meet a nebulous standard. The Revised Version (1881) translation better conveys Paul's meaning: "But let a man prove himself, and so let him eat of the bread and drink of the cup."
- The following illustrates the point in a different way, and is worth repeating:

> This story has been told of the famous Scottish theologian John Duncan, of New College in Edinburgh. At communion one Sunday, when the elements came to a sixteen-year-old girl, she suddenly turned her head aside. She motioned for the elder to take the cup away, that she couldn't drink it. John Duncan reached his long arm over, touched her shoulder and said tenderly, "Take it lassie, it's for sinners!"[194]

6. *Because one expression of love is hospitality—which includes treating others as we'd want to be treated in their situation:*
   - "So in everything, do to others what you would have them do to you, for this sums up the Law and the Prophets" (Matthew 7:12, NIV).
   - "Practice hospitality" (Romans 12:13b, NIV).

7. *Because any discipline believers suffer from participating in the Lord's Supper in an unworthy manner is intended to be redemptive (for our good) and it's only believers who will be disciplined:*

---

194 Michael Green, ed., *Illustrations for Biblical Preaching* (Grand Rapids, Michigan: Baker Book House, 1989), 75.

• "And have you forgotten the encouraging words God spoke to you as his children? He said, 'My child, don't make light of the LORD's discipline, and don't give up when he corrects you. For the LORD disciplines those he loves, and he punishes each one he accepts as his child.' As you endure this divine discipline, remember that God is treating you as his own children. Who ever heard of a child who is never disciplined by its father? If God doesn't discipline you as he does all of his children, it means that you are illegitimate and are not really his children at all. Since we respected our earthly fathers who disciplined us, shouldn't we submit even more to the discipline of the Father of our spirits, and live forever?" (Hebrews 12:5–9, NLT).

Certainly I respect those who've thought this question through biblically and come to a different conclusion. George Patterson's perspective can be seen as a rebuttal to the points above:

It does cheapen the sacrament's significance, however, if we let everyone and anyone take it; it is one of the most sacred things a church body can do. So, if unsaved visitors are present, I recommend not offending them by saying things like, "You can't take part."

Rather, you can signal to them not to take the sacrament by saying something like, "This is a very sacred thing that believers in Christ do. If you are not yet a believer, then please observe carefully, because it's our prayer and hope that you will soon, maybe even now, join us in our faith and fellowship."[195]

---

195   George Patterson, email message to author, Nov. 24, 2014.

I would counter that we have to take initiative to ensure we don't hide the meal from outsiders and make it an insider event rather than a proclamation of truth relevant for all humankind. Certainly the Holy Spirit may guide a leader in a particular setting to make an appeal for repentance in connection with communion,

A variation of Patterson's response is to see the Lord's Supper as a "covenant feast," restricted to those who are part of the covenant. Yet, the three primary covenant feasts of the Hebrew people: Passover, and Pentecost (or Harvest), and Tabernacles (or Shelters), had specific instructions providing for including outsiders:

> And if foreigners living among you want to celebrate the Passover to the Lord, they must follow these same decrees and regulations. The same laws apply both to native-born Israelites and to the foreigners living among you.[196]

> Count off seven weeks from when you first begin to cut the grain at the time of harvest. Then celebrate the Festival of Harvest to honor the Lord your God. Bring him a voluntary offering in proportion to the blessings you have received

---

196 Numbers 9:14, NLT. This instruction clarifies Exodus 12:43–49 (NLT), which at first glance could seem restrictive: "Then the Lord said to Moses and Aaron, 'These are the instructions for the festival of Passover. No outsiders are allowed to eat the Passover meal. But any slave who has been purchased may eat it if he has been circumcised. Temporary residents and hired servants may not eat it. Each Passover lamb must be eaten in one house. Do not carry any of its meat outside, and do not break any of its bones. The whole community of Israel must celebrate this Passover festival. If there are foreigners living among you who want to celebrate the Lord's Passover, let all their males be circumcised. Only then may they celebrate the Passover with you like any native-born Israelite. But no uncircumcised male may ever eat the Passover meal. This instruction applies to everyone, whether a native-born Israelite or a foreigner living among you.'"

from him. This is a time to celebrate before the Lord your God at the designated place of worship he will choose for his name to be honored. Celebrate with your sons and daughters, your male and female servants, the Levites from your towns, and the foreigners, orphans, and widows who live among you. Remember that you were once slaves in Egypt, so be careful to obey all these decrees.

"You must observe the Festival of Shelters for seven days at the end of the harvest season, after the grain has been threshed and the grapes have been pressed. This festival will be a happy time of celebrating with your sons and daughters, your male and female servants, and the Levites, foreigners, orphans, and widows from your towns.[197]

- Author John Sandford raises a different concern about an open approach: Since we are receiving the cup of forgiveness, doesn't everyone participating need to be walking in the reality of that? That sounds reasonable—until I try to start measuring—have I forgiven that person "enough"? Paul's instructions were to prove, approve, or examine one's *own* self in receiving communion. The instructions weren't for leaders to set performance or "heart" standards for others before they could participate.

---

197   Deuteronomy 16:9–14, NLT.

CELEBRATING COMMUNION IN A MEAL

THERE HAVE BEEN occasional reappearances of at least part of what the early church enjoyed. Many believers can remember times of spiritual refreshing, and also recall meals or time together over food as part of those times. It may simply have been dessert at a restaurant together after amazing Sunday evening services. However, in our day those times aren't usually connected to a conscious recognition of the body and blood of our Lord.

John Wesley adapted a practice he'd seen in the Moravian movement for the societies he set up. He said:

> In order to increase in [persons in these Methodist soci-
> eties] a grateful sense of all God's mercies, I desired that
> one evening in a quarter all men in band, on a second all
> the women, would meet, and on a third both men and
> women together, that we might together "eat bread," as
> the ancient Christians did, "with gladness and single-
> ness of heart." At these love-feasts (so we termed them,
> retaining the name as well as the thing, which was in
> use from the beginning) our food is only a little plain

cake and water; but we seldom return from them without being fed not only with the "meat which perisheth," but with "that which endureth to everlasting life."[198]

Methodist historian Dr. Frank Baker said the loss of this practice was because love feasts were "a product and instrument of revivalism."[199]

"A product and instrument of revivalism!" Is that the simple reason for the original Lord's Supper being replaced by a shorter ceremony in the second- and third-century church? As one generation passed the faith on to another and "human traditions" sometimes took an upper hand, was such decay inevitable?

To ensure we explore this issue fully, let me give a couple of other perspectives.

George Patterson reports that contemporary church-planting movements that have combined a meal with the Lord's Supper end up dropping the meal because people become too focused on the food. He would see Paul's words "if anyone is hungry, let him eat at home" as directive, asking us to focus on simply the bread and the cup.[200] (I would see them as permissive!) At the other end of the spectrum, Verlon Fosner has been part of and observed a movement of gatherings based around a meal. These "dinner churches" feature a meal for the marginalized, the poor and the lonely where Jesus is lifted up in different simple forms, such as through reading a parable at the beginning of the meal, and offering for the guests to stay and discuss it afterwards. A few of these dinner

---

198 *Free Methodist Church. Pastor's Handbook* (Indianapolis, Indiana: Light and Life Communications, 1998), 41–42. The focus of the Methodist love feast included reconciliation of members one with another. The book goes on to say: "Although the observance of the love feast has declined in Free Methodism in recent years, where it has been re-introduced it provides the church an opportunity to maintain 'singleness of heart' through forgiving love which overcomes petty differences or misunderstandings."

199 Ibid.

200 Personal conversation with the author, July 17, 2014.

gatherings consciously share the bread and the cup, most don't. But all of these gatherings can be described as "table-focused" churches rather than a teaching and performance gathering.[201]

Keith Watkins sees the elimination of any eating connected with the Lord's Supper as a purification:

> There came a time, probably before the close of the New Testament period, when the meal became even more highly stylized. The natural side of it, the eating and drinking, was suppressed in order to let the new meaning be expressed without confusion or possible misunderstanding. People ceased to eat the full meal and instead partook only of the bread and wine used in the ritual of remembrance and praise.[202]

He goes on to explain why he sees this as a good change:

> Because a normal meal is a time for eating, we want short prayers and minimal extraneous ceremony. Because the Lord's Supper is a time for remembering Jesus and praising God, we do not want to be distracted by much eating. It may be that this is the reason why the efforts to recombine the Lord's Supper and a regular meal turn out to be so clumsy and unsatisfying. The food confuses the ceremonial side of our gathering, just as the ceremony would inhibit the enjoyment of a meal.[203]

---

201 See *DinnerChurchCollective.net* including Verlon Fosner, *Welcome to Dinner, Church*, an 88-page book introducing Jesus' dinner table theology with a discussion guide for groups getting ready to start a Dinner Church.

202 Keith Watkins, *The Feast of Joy* (St. Louis, Missouri: Bethany Press, 1977), 18.

203 Ibid. I would suggest the Lord's Supper should be more than "a time for remembering Jesus and praising God"—much more!

But a short ceremony sandwiched in between other elements of a church meeting can be unsatisfying as well! Earlier in his book, Watkins likened the Lord's Supper to a birthday party in U.S. culture.[204] There's a sameness and familiarity to the candles, the cake, and singing a song, just as there's a repetition time after time of sharing the cup and the bread.

Let's develop that comparison. If all there is to a party is cake, candles, and a song, the birthday honoree is shortchanged! For a real party, there's got to be something more—some emotional connection, some food, some time to talk and relate. I've been part of the obligatory workplace birthday party for a co-worker I hardly knew. Surely they're unsatisfying for everyone involved! Why? Because they're an outward show with little inward reality.

To me, a supper for a loving God-man is short on religious form and long on relational substance. (I'm saying "is" deliberately! I'm speaking of truth, not commenting or recording our experience.)

Does returning the cup and the bread to the context of a real meal have to be "unsatisfying?" I was awoken to the possibility that a real meal can be part of our celebration by an American who spent some time in India, Richard Slimbach. He told me about being part of an indigenous church movement there during the early 1980s:

> Every Sunday Bakht Singh [the leader] or one of his associates would lead not one, but two communion ceremonies which were embedded within a four-hour-long service. After several indigenous-styled hymns he would direct congregants' attention to the passion of Christ through scripture and illustration. Then, after the elements were passed, he would lead the congregation in perhaps 30–45 minutes of intercession in which he would recall, without the aid of notes, the names and needs of

204   Ibid, 15.

other associates (church planters) worldwide. Again, this would take place twice during a given Sunday service.

Following the service, there would be a community feast (we're talking 2,000 people), and then a procession throughout the city. Remember, the majority of these congregants were simple, unlearned folk but "rich toward God" in ways unknown to most Westerners.[205]

Simply hearing about such an event awakened something in me—there's more available than I've experienced.

Certainly Passover is celebrated as a full meal—not a short ceremonial token reception of lamb and wine. Why is Passover more "satisfying" as a practice than the contemporary efforts to combine the Lord's Supper with a meal? Part of it is no doubt the ceremonial content, the script. The Lord's Supper can be done so briefly and simply that our minds can wander and become focused on other things as the meal goes on. A liturgy like the one contained in Appendix 4 would be one way to combat this, and bring about some of the same depth as the Passover *haggadah* (script) has.

Is it possible that the Lord's Supper is a key battleground, as we attempt to renew our minds and see all of life as sacred, as connected to Jesus? It isn't just the meal of a cracker or wafer and the cup that's sacred—it's all our meals eaten under his Lordship. In a loving family, birthday parties are special, but they're part of a pattern of connection—connections which include eating together at other times besides birthdays.

So how can we start restoring the fullness of the Lord's Supper? Do we only celebrate it in the context of a church covered-dish meal?

Or can we start taking baby steps in another direction? Could we, when we're enjoying a meal with other believers, take some time to focus on the Lord through sharing the bread and the cup?

---

205 Richard Slimbach, email to the author, March 30, 2005.

It's possible of course that we need the horse before the cart, in line with what Frank Baker said about love feasts being a product of Holy Spirit visitation. *As the church is brought to life, as the Holy Spirit fills us, then sharing the Lord through the bread and the cup at a meal will become a natural (or supernatural!) result. The importance of "breaking of bread" will be restored just in the normal course of church life.* When people are hungry for the Lord, for obeying His every direction, they'll look for occasions to celebrate Him in the bread and the cup. Whether it's a small group, covered dish meal, or an evening with friends, it seems such events could be closest to what Acts 2:42 and 2:46 speak of—and we can pray the spirit and fruit would be a blessed and holy unity.

APPENDIX 3

WHAT COULD IT BE LIKE?

"WE FOUND IN Rhode Island that the celebration of the Lord's Table is very valuable for new churches. We encourage them to make the celebration meaningful."[206] These words of Bob Scroggins, from his advice to those leading house churches, actually show the challenge we face. How do we "make" something meaningful? The Lord's Supper has such amazing intrinsic meaning, we shouldn't need to "make the celebration meaning-ful"—but evidently we do! The meaning has apparently been watered down and diluted. Perhaps Scroggins was noticing that sometimes repeating an action the same way all the time can lead to a familiarity which breeds boredom (but hopefully not contempt) rather than being an encouraging event which communicates unity and being at home with our God.

Or perhaps he was getting at something specific: How do we make communion a time where people connect relationally with one another? Given many established traditions and patterns, it takes thought and advance preparation to set an atmosphere that gets people to connect at the same time we're sharing the bread and the cup. It can involve the hard work of creative thinking—but isn't it worth the same amount of advance work as a music set or a sermon involves? This does appear to be what Scroggins was getting at, as he went on to say:

---

206   Bob Scroggins, and George Patterson, *Church Multiplication Guide*, revised edi-tion (Pasadena, California: William Carey Library, 2002), 71.

Often we celebrate it as part of an event of importance for the church community. Such an event is when new members are being "covenanted" into the church. Another is when we send members off to start a new congregation, or when two or more of our churches meet together. . . .

We often have the Lord's Table around a fellowship meal. Sometimes we do it at the beginning of the meal, other times at the end. Still other times we have the bread at the beginning and the cup at the end, symbolizing our communion with the Lord throughout the meal. . . . We consciously avoid a single pattern, preferring a "menu" approach; the one who leads the ceremony prayerfully considers suitable options for activities that make the experience more meaningful.[207]

So how does one connect people with both the joy of our Lord and one another? Here are some ideas:

Common cup—dipping the bread: In our germ-conscious culture, how do we get back to the common cup? One way, in the context of a small group, or multiple small groups, is "intinction." Have a cup or bowl and have each person dip the bread in it and receive both in that form. (If it's a small group, it may be possible to arrange to have everyone dip their bread simultaneously into a broad bowl of grape juice, which emphasizes that we are one body.)

Chain communion: Each person in a group administers the bread and the cup to the next person, in turn. They can be coached on what to say, like, "The body and blood of our Lord given for you."

"Discerning the Body" communion: Explain Paul's concern that the richer believers in Corinth needed to recognize their unity with those in financial need. Offer people a practical way of expressing their concern.

This could be giving an offering for those in need as they approach the table to receive the elements (or picking up an envelope for a future offering).

Releasing offenses communion: Invite people to a communion/potluck. Sit around tables and have a short time of musical worship. Give an explanation of how it's helpful to do something specific to release specific offenses one has experienced that are keeping one unsettled. Ask people to write something about the offense down on a card, fold it, and bring it up to a wooden cross. Provide hammers and nails for each person to nail their folded card to the cross. (The card should be folded so we don't increase any offenses if someone happens to read something in someone else's card!)

The host at each table then shares the bread and cup around the table—and following that, a potluck meal is served. Since many children will finish before their parents, give them the fun task of tearing the folded cards off the cross and putting them into a paper shredder!

Enter into the spirit of the Last Supper: Set a time, possibly Maundy Thursday[208] or Good Friday evening. Have twelve men sitting or reclining around a raised platform/table, dressed in first-century garb. For visibility this could be on a raised stage. In order to partake, people approach the table and then are served the bread and the cup by the men. The "disciples" who serve can share something briefly or pray for the person receiving the bread and cup.

Connecting with Passover ceremony: Explain the reason for including children is based in part because of the context of the Last Supper—the Passover ceremony. Have a young child come and ask the question which is a key part of that ceremony: "What makes this night different than every other night?"

---

208   "Maundy Thursday" is the name given to the Thursday before Good Friday. Some churches have well-developed liturgies to remember the Last Supper. The term "maundy" comes from the Latin word which shows up in English as "mandate"—the adjective is referring to Jesus' command to "Do this in remembrance of me."

"What makes this moment different than every other moment? It's different because we are recognizing and remembering how our Lord has delivered us!"

"My story" time: Another communion potluck, with the focus being on the different ways the Lord reaches people. Have a few people share their testimony stories, and then ask each table to share their testimony stories in a similar way around their table. Then each table host shares the bread and the cup. After that, a regular meal—with an atmosphere no doubt charged with the thanksgiving and delight over the different ways our Lord reaches people.

Christmas & Easter Combined: I'm indebted to Pastor Clyde Owens for this approach. He would dress as a street person and do a silent pantomime (with background music and sound effects) for an audience. He would come and discover a gift—that turned out to be, evidently, a baby wrapped in a cloth. He would be quite delighted, hugging and kissing the baby. Then as the sound effects change from music to thunder, he proceeds to nail the wrapped baby to a cross—and then as he unwraps it, it turns out to be a loaf of bread, which he shares with each person there. (He would also give out a squarish nail, dipped in red paint to each person taking part.) He wanted to communicate that the best way we can understand the innocence of the man who was nailed to the cross is to think of a baby!

Mobius Strip communion: This mathematical puzzle (named after one of the two 19th century German mathematicians who discovered it) can portray what happens in the action of us sharing our Lord's body and blood. Prepare a strip of paper for each person taking part—label one side "Jesus' blood" and the other side "Our Cup." At one end of the strip, put a piece of double-sided tape. Instruct the participants to twist the end of the strip without the tape once and then tape it onto the end (and side) with the tape. The simple action of twisting and joining the ends makes it a continuous loop. It changes from being two-sided, with four edges, to one-sided with one continuous edge.

Proclaim the good news out among people: This may be a stretch for some, but if the Lord is being proclaimed through the action of sharing the cup and bread—then why not consider what was done in Sweden:

> [A] couple of Lutheran priests created church for the marginalized of society. They gather on a weekday in a busy city-centre square. In full view of all the passing shoppers, they don sacramental robes, set a trestle table as an altar, covering it with embroidered cloth and lighted candles. Then with guitars and formal Eucharistic liturgy they draw the homeless, addicts, prostitutes and punks and offer blessed bread and wine. These are the disenfranchised who would never enter a church building on a Sunday—which to them is the *form* that carries the *meaning* of all the oppressive power systems that push them to the bottom. But Christendom is also still strong enough for the *meanings* of bread and wine to speak of a Saviour who accepts them and gave his life for them. . . . Those that respond regularly are drawn into a small discipling community in a nearby rented shop-front, where their worldview and values are rebuilt around the biblical revelation.[209]

Introduce a past liturgy: Use a script for the ceremony from someone who's gone before us. This may unnerve some contemporary believers. In fact, I heard this comment addressed to one leader who took this step: "Just don't start wearing a robe!" Yet these scripts or liturgies connect us to the stream of history all believers share. (See next appendix for a possibility.)

---

209 Bob Hopkins and Mike Breen, *Clusters: Creative Mid-sized Missional Communities* (Sheffield, United Kingdom: 3dmpublishing, 2007) 126–127.

The Cup of Thanksgiving: Paul refers to the cup with this term in 1 Corinthians 10:16. Based on this, share the communion cup using the part of the Jewish Passover ceremony which is sometime termed "the cup of thanksgiving" (the third of the four cups which are part of the Passover ceremony). Following a prayer of thanksgiving and this blessing, "Blessed are you, O Lord our God, King of the universe, who has created the fruit of the vine," the third cup would be drunk. This would be followed by singing (or have different people read them) the second part of the Hallel (Psalms 115–118), followed by "The Great Hallel," Psalm 136.

Couples serving one another: Don and Bernadette Haddleton offered the elements to everyone at their renewal of vows ceremony—asking husbands and wives to dip the chunk of bread in the cup—and then to put it simultaneously in their spouse's mouth.

The Conception Community Farm celebration: This can be done, as I learned from Bobbie and Jenn Wright and their group in urban Kansas City, by sharing the cup and bread before a community supper. Start with a bottle of grape juice or wine and a goblet in a bowl. Each member shares something specific he or she is thankful for, in turn. After a person shares, they pour a small amount into the goblet from the bottle. The last one to share pours in enough so the goblet overflows. (This part is reminiscent of part of the *Havdalah,* the ceremony that ends the Jewish Sabbath.) The whole group sings a song, and the host prays. Then the bread is shared around the circle, with each person saying to the next in turn as they pass it: "The body of our Lord given for you." After everyone's had some bread, there's a moment of silence. Then following a prayer, the cup is passed. Each person gives thanks for something different than they had said the first round. This is followed by another moment of silence and a final prayer. There's a natural transition into the meal with the food either already on the table or served immediately.

Meditate on the relationship: This framework can be used with various artistic expressions related to the Lord's Supper, whether songs, stories, or visual art. For instance, one could play the song "The Wrote and

the Writ" by Johnnie Flynn as a way to encourage those who are receiving the Lord's Supper to enter into the mystery. The song contains lyrics
that could refer to a disappointed lover, or possibly be about one's relationship with God. This may surface issues like, "My connection with
God is just His written word—I don't feel Him in my heart!" Then you
can receive the bread and the cup.[210]

Consider the unspoken message of one's approach: I brought up with
the pastors on our team: "Every time we celebrate the Lord's Supper we
reinforce the idea that you have to be a pastor to lead it!" Don't we want
believers to initiate obeying Jesus, not passively wait for others or "the
church schedule?" How do we get from here to there? As a first step,
model having the Lord's Supper in small groups—at a regular service.
Prepare trays of cups and bread, enough for ten to twelve people; and
then have people divide up into groups. Explain how to share the Supper, and then invite one person from each group (you can appoint them
with some direction like the person who most recently had a birthday) to
come get a tray and share it with their group. Then this can be followed
on a different occasion by asking everyone in a congregation to celebrate
the Supper with their household on a particular evening.

One great teacher of teachers, Howard Hendricks, was quoted as saying, "If you are going to bore people, don't bore them with the Gospel. Bore
them with calculus, bore them with earth science. . . . But it is a sin to bore
people with the Gospel."[211] Surely the same is true for the Lord's Supper!

210   *"The Wrote and the Writ"* by John Patrick Vivian Flynn. Song lyrics © Warner/
      Chappell Music, Inc, 2008. This song uses the Lord's Supper as a motif.
211   Quoted in Lawrence O. Richards and Gary J. Bredfeldt, *Creative Bible Teaching,*
      revised edition (Chicago: Moody Press, 1998), 218.

SCRIPT FOR A COMMUNION SERVICE

THIS COMMUNION SERVICE is based on one by Balthasar Hübmaier, martyred along with his wife by the Austrian monarchy in Vienna, 1528. Hübmaier was a theologian during the Reformation, who "had moved to pastor the church at Waldshut, in Austria, where he began experimenting with ways to bring that parish into the deeper faith that he had become convinced was necessary to be a true disciple of Christ. He broke the rules of the mass, offering the cup to the common people—and this brought him into conflict with the Bishop of Constance."[212]

SCRIPT

OPENING & WELCOME TO ALL

MUSICAL PRAISE & WORSHIP

CONFESSION *(everyone say in unison while kneeling or taking another appropriate physical attitude):*
Father, we have sinned against heaven and against You. We aren't

---

212   Biography adapted from House Church Central website, http://www.hccentral.
com/gkeys/hbmier.html.

worthy to be called Your children. But besides originally creating us, You have redeemed us back to Yourself, adopted us as Your children, and are making us whole!

Thank you almighty, eternal, gracious God for being gracious to us and having mercy on us sinners.

Thank You for bringing us into living relationship with You, which is eternal life; and thank You for the assurance that we will dwell in eternity with You, through Jesus Christ our Lord and Savior. Amen. *(People sit.)*

SCRIPTURE READING AND EXPLANATION: *John 13 & 14 or similar passages*

- *Response to Scripture (individually or corporately at tables)*
- *Open testimony & water baptism (if appropriate)*
- *Testimony around tables*

PRAYER *(in unison)*:

Stay with us, O Christ! It is toward evening, and the day is now far spent. Abide with us, O Jesus; abide with us. For where You are not, there everything is darkness, night, and shadow. But You alone are the true Son, light and shining brightness. Those for whom You light the way, they cannot go astray.

SELF-EXAMINATION *(in unison)*:

Let us prove ourselves as we approach the Lord's Supper:

Do I believe utterly and absolutely that Christ gave His body and shed His crimson blood for us on the cross?

Do I fervently hunger for the bread which comes down from heaven?

Do I thirst for the drink which flows into eternal life?

Do I desire to eat and drink in the spirit, faith, and truth which Christ teaches us?

Am I thankful both in words and in deeds toward God, for the abundant and unspeakable love and goodness shown through our Lord Jesus Christ?

Am I willing to say this publicly, and if it be the Lord's will am I willing to offer my body and blood for my Lord and my fellow believers?

EXHORTATION *(by leader)*:

To fulfill the law, it is not enough to avoid sins and die to them. For we are called not only to forsake evil but to do good. We are called to do good to our neighbor. For Christ not only broke the bread, he also gave it to his disciples. And not only the bread, but also His own flesh and blood. So we must not only speak the word of love, hear it, confess ourselves to be sinners, and abstain from sin. We must fulfill love in deeds, as Scripture everywhere teaches us. In sum, God requires of us the will, the word, and the works of love. God will not be paid off or dismissed with words.

Silence—followed by prayers of the people, concluding with the Lord's Prayer (in unison):

Our Father, who art in heaven, hallowed be Your name. Let Your kingship come, let Your will be done on earth as it is in heaven. Give us this day our daily bread. Forgive us for the ways we have wronged You, just as we also forgive those who have wronged us. And lead us not into temptation but deliver us from evil.[213]

EXPRESSION OF LOVE:

Leader: The Lord Jesus, on the night He was betrayed, said that He had desired to eat this supper with His friends with an intense desire. Whoever now desires to eat this bread and drink this cup of the Lord's Supper, let us rise and respond with heart and mouth and express the desires of our Lord for us.

(All stand.)

---

213 Translation from combined sources.

Brothers and sisters, if you desire to love God before, in, and above all things, in the power of His holy and living Word; if you desire to serve, honor, and adore God, and to sanctify His name; and to subject your sinful will to God's divine will which He has worked in you by the living Word, then let each say individually, "I desire it."

People: I desire it.

Leader: If you desire to love and serve your neighbor with deeds of love, to lay down for him or her your life; if you desire to honor your father and mother, and submit to and obey all authorities according to the will of God, and this in the power of our Lord Jesus Christ, who laid down His flesh and blood for us, then let each say individually, "I desire it."

People: I desire it.

Leader: If you desire to practice straightforward communication, including correction when necessary, toward your brothers and sisters; make peace and unity among them; and reconcile yourselves with all whom you have offended; if you desire to abandon all envy, hate, and evil will toward others, and willingly cease all action and behavior which causes harm, disadvantage, or offense to your neighbor; if you will love your enemies and do good to them, then let each say individually, "I desire it."

People: I desire it.

Leader: If you desire publicly to confirm before the church this expression of love which you have now made, through the Lord's Supper, by eating bread and drinking of the cup, and to testify to it in the power of the living memorial of the suffering and death of Jesus Christ our Lord, then let each say individually, "I desire it in the power of God."

People: I desire it in the power of God.

Leader: So eat and drink with one another in the name of God the Father, the Son, and the Holy Spirit. May God accord to all of us the power and the strength that we may worthily carry out His desires and see His kingship expressed more fully here on earth. May the Lord Jesus impart to us His grace. Amen.

THANKSGIVING: *(As congregation continues to stand, leader takes the bread; all in congregation lift their eyes and pray.)*

People: We praise and thank you, Lord God, Creator of the heavens and earth, for all Your goodness toward us. Especially we thank You that You so sincerely loved us and gave Your most beloved Son for us, so that we who believe in Jesus may not be lost, but have eternal life. May You be honored, praised, and magnified now, forever, always, and eternally. Amen.

MUSICAL WORSHIP

BREAKING AND DISTRIBUTION OF BREAD:

Leader (breaking the bread): The Lord Jesus, in the night in which He was betrayed, took the bread, gave thanks, broke it, and said: "Take, eat. This is my body which is broken for you. Do this in my memory." Therefore, dear brothers and sisters, take, and eat also this bread in the memory of the body of our Lord Jesus Christ, which He gave unto death for us.

(Leader offers the bread into the hands of those present; people hold their fragment of bread, and then eat it together.)

SHARING OF THE CUP:

Leader (taking cup, speaking with lifted eyes):

God! Praise be to you! Likewise, the Lord Jesus took the cup after Supper and said: "This cup is a new testament in my blood. Do this, as often as you drink, in memory of me." Take, therefore, also the cup, and all drink from it in the memory of the blood of our Lord Jesus Christ, which was shed for us for the forgiveness of our sins. *(Leader passes the cup to the people, and all drink. Offer individual cups for people who wish.)*

People: As often as we eat the bread and drink of the drink, we proclaim the death of the Lord, until He comes. *(People sit down.)*

CONCLUSION:

Leader: By eating the bread and sharing the cup in memory of the suffering and shed blood of our Lord Jesus Christ for the remission of our sins, we have had fellowship with one another. By eating the bread and sharing the cup in the Lord's memory, we have all demonstrated we are one loaf and one body. Our Head is Christ. We are called to be conformed to our Head and as his members to follow after him. We are called to love one another, to do good, to give counsel, and to be helpful to one another, each offering up our flesh and blood for the other.

And so I urge you, most dearly beloved in Christ, as table companions of Christ Jesus, to lead a Christian walk before God and all people. Remember to express your love to our Lord through obedience. Bear fruit worthy of the baptism and the Supper of Christ. May you in the power of God continue in your commitment to His Lordship. God sees and knows our hearts. May our Lord Jesus Christ, ever and eternally praised, grant us the same. Amen.

Dear brothers and sisters, watch and pray, lest you wander away and fall into temptation. We know neither the day nor the hour when the Lord is coming and will ask an accounting of our life. Therefore, watch and pray. I commend you to God. May all of us say,

People: Praise, praise, praise to the Lord eternally! Amen.

Leader: And so let us rise. *(People stand.)* Go in the peace of Christ Jesus.

People: The grace of God be with us all. Amen.

Another source for a communion liturgy that gives substantial time to the ceremony is the Northumbria Community (northumbriacommunity. org): "Northumbria Community is a dispersed network of people, hugely diverse, from different backgrounds, streams and edges of the Christian faith. . . [W]e are united in our desire to embrace and express an ongoing exploration into a new way for living, through a new monasticism."

IS BREAKING BREAD ONE OF TWO FORMS OF FELLOWSHIP?

"And they devoted themselves to the apostles'
teaching and the fellowship, to the breaking
of bread and the prayers."[214]

IMAGINE THIS—SOMETHING as arcane as the grammar of this sentence in Acts can confirm the key role of the Lord's Supper.

This verse is a summary of the life the very first church enjoyed, so it gets referred to again and again by those looking to understand what's crucial for our life together as believers.

How does the grammar confirm the Lord's Supper's importance? Here's a sentence with the same grammatical construction, where the final clause is a description of the final word in the previous phrase: "They visited Mexico and the United States, California, and Oregon."[215] California and Oregon are the parts of the United States they visited.

---

214 Acts 2:42, ESV.

215 I recognize there are a couple of understandings of how to interpret the Greek grammar here. I'm indebted to Steve Carpenter, "The Lord's Supper" audio CD (Kansas City, Missouri: Friends of the Bridegroom, Oct. 2003), for first alerting me to this understanding. Other interpretations include seeing "fellowship" (Greek *koinonia*) as a meal separate from the Lord's Supper, or as referring to the sharing of resources which is described in detail a short time later in Luke's account. However, the most common alternative is to see "fellowship" as the second item in a list of four activities—and simply avoid the question, "What did the fellowship consist of?" That's why the understanding I present, which sees an explanation of the word "fellowship" coming immediately after the word is used, seems superior to me.

Similarly, the "breaking of bread" here is a subset of fellowship (or *koinonia*). [216] "Breaking of bread" isn't different from *fellowship*; but is one of the two parts of *fellowship*, one of the two ways we partner with one another and the Lord.

For years I saw a fourfold description of church life in Acts 2:42: apostles teaching, fellowship, breaking of bread, and the prayers. I saw "fellowship" as chatting with fellow believers and the "breaking of bread" as the ceremony of the Lord's Supper—two completely distinct things. I'm all for talking to other believers; how can we be in real partnership without doing so? But it appears that the fellowship the early church had with one another (and our Lord) consisted of two activities: praying together and sharing food, and the Lord's Supper, together. (Even if you stick with understanding "fellowship" as a separate category from "the breaking of bread," the latter is still obviously important!) This understanding of the grammar emphasizes the utmost priority of the Lord's Supper.

---

216   "The term *koinonia* is found only here in all of Luke-Acts, though the idea is
      common. The term itself means a participation or sharing in common of some-
      thing with someone else, in this case eating and praying. Thus, fellowship is not
      a very helpful translation, for fellowship is the result of *koinonia*, of sharing in
      common; it is not the *koinonia* itself. *Koinonia* is an activity which can result in
      fellowship of some sort, and it can entail things like sharing not just spiritual
      activities such as prayer but also physical food or other goods." Ben Withering-
      ton III, *The Acts of the Apostles: A Socio-Rhetorical Commentary* (Grand Rapids,
      Michigan: Eerdmans, 1998), 160.

_____

THE BREAD AND THE CUP

The bread and the cup
Such a fragile weapon
Compared to a sword
Such a weak defense
Against a foe like suicide
Such a thin argument
Confronting scientism
Such an obscure action
Compared to entertainment
Yet fragile like a spider's web
Enduring through rain and poison
Weak like an invalid
Who lives to be a 100
Thin like a strand of glass
Connecting continents
Obscure like yeast particles
Expanding on and on and on.
—DAVID WARNICK

_____

CONTACT THE AUTHOR

David Warnick
Look to the Lord
PO Box 2168
Hayden, Idaho 83835

dwarnick@newlifeid.com